Becoming a Tour Guide

Also available:
Forsyth: *Career Skills*
Hamilton: *Passing Exams*
Knight: *The Secretary's Software Survival Guide*
Neidle: *How to Get into Advertising*

Verité Reily Collins

Becoming a Tour Guide

Principles of guiding and site interpretation

continuum
LONDON • NEW YORK

Continuum

The Tower Building
11 York Road
London SE1 7NX
www.continuumbooks.com

370 Lexington Avenue
New York
NY 10017–6503

First published 2000

Reprinted 2002

British Library Cataloguing-in-Publication Data
A catalogue record for this book is available from the British Library.

ISBN: 0 8264 4788 0

Typeset by Centraserve, Saffron Walden, Essex
Printed in Great Britain by Biddles Ltd *www.biddles.co.uk*

Contents

	Acknowledgements	vii
	Introduction	ix
1	Different types of work	1
2	Tour managers	13
3	Guides	22
4	Planning your working day	38
5	Training	44
6	Running a training course	66
7	Finding work	74
8	Interviews	81
9	Working with colleagues	86
10	Working with clients	98
11	Making life easier	104
12	Why don't we . . .?	114
13	Working from home	122
14	Looking after yourself	127
15	Associations	131
16	Stocking your bookshelf	134
17	Helpful contacts	139
	Glossary	144
	Index	145

Acknowledgements

Richard Allen of the English Tourism Council; Alan Bowen; Donna Bridgland; Sigrid Griffiths; Ron Jones and Eva Dix of the International Association of Tour Managers; Jane Orde; Michelle Ramsey; Doreen Boyle and Christine Wade of the Scottish Tourist Guides Association; Val Wooff; the staff of Brompton Library, Chelsea; and all the colleagues and friends who allowed themselves to be quoted, and gave helpful advice.

Introduction

Welcome to tourism, the world's fastest expanding and probably largest industry, dedicated to encouraging people to travel for pleasure and business. These travellers often need people to look after them, popularly described as tour guides. This description mixes two job titles: tour manager and tour guide.

Tour managers accompany groups anywhere in the world, travelling with their clients and usually staying in the same place as clients until the end of the tour.

Guides generally work in one area or region, returning to their home each night.

Tour managers and guides play an increasingly important role in tourism, not only carrying out the administration and 'handling' clients booked with a tour operator, but also acting as the interface between visitors and locals.

We all want to travel and see other regions and countries. We all tend to think of ourselves as travellers, and other visitors as tourists. Tourism can be a force for good, injecting new ideas, impressions and money into the local infrastructure. However, unless handled intelligently, the most sympathetic tourists are frequently suspected of bringing with them a 'battering ram' approach to local sights and customs.

So apart from looking after clients on behalf of their companies, tour managers and guides will be playing an increasingly important role as the interface between visitors and locals, ensuring visitors enjoy their visit but don't upset the local ecology.

Once, you were thrown into this work without proper training. Now, because of the EU Directive on Package Travel, tour operators have a duty of care to their clients, so should ensure staff are well trained. This book outlines some of the training available, from small private courses, official tourist boards and NVQs, and where to find this.

The tourist profile is changing, and staff need to ensure that visitors see and experience new areas, without disrupting local life. Today, training should encourage a partnership approach between locals, tour managers and guides, and visitors. The recent TV series *Tourist Trouble* showed the outcome of some 'old-fashioned' training at its worst, but new initiatives are set to encourage a more informed and ecologically sound approach to welcoming visitors.

Most tour managers and guides work as freelances; it is very, very unusual to be employed full-time. So if you are not able to handle the loneliness and frustrations of being your own boss – perhaps this work is not for you?

Age is almost immaterial; if you enjoy your job and can enthuse your audience, you will find work from the age of 16 to 75 and over.

If you like meeting people, helping them and seeing what makes them tick, the work is fascinating and incredibly satisfying: where else are you thanked at the end of the day, just for doing your job?

As you read through the book, we have asked Sam, Valerie, Sophie, Sigrid, Tom, Arthur, Mark and Charlie to tell you about their working days: the frustrations, problems, tears – and triumphs.

1 Different types of work

There are two strands of work in this sector of the tourism industry: tour managing and guiding.

Tour managers

Accompanying groups or individual clients travelling on a holiday, or on a business trip, involving overnight stays, tour managers are responsible for the administration and smooth running of the tour for its duration, and generally stay with the group.

Guides

Guides work on site or in an area for an hour, a half-day or a full day, or even for several days with the same individuals or groups, returning to their base every evening. If a guide is booked for several days, generally they return home at the end of the working day, rather than stay with their visitors.

Work can involve taking individuals or groups

- on foot – e.g. walking-tour guides, site guides, museum guides, trail guides, 'interpreters'
- on coaches
- using cycles or even horses for transport (an expanding sector)
- using your own car as a car-driver guide, or accompanying clients in a chauffeur-driven limousine. This is not to be confused with coach drivers guiding as they drive, which is illegal (see Chapter 9)

What do the jobs involve?

Perhaps the easiest way to have some idea of the work involved is to ask Valerie and Sophie to describe their working day. Valerie is an experienced tour manager; Sophie an experienced guide. When asked, both said there is no typical day – every day is different. However, they agreed a day in their working lives might go something like this:

Valerie the tour manager

Before meeting clients at the start of a tour I will have checked all documentation, tickets, vouchers, passenger and rooming lists, lists of hotels, restaurant stops, contact phone numbers for the office, local guides, coach company, etc. and collected a cheque for the float.

I then go over the itinerary carefully, checking again that I have all the relevant paperwork and contact telephone numbers. I then go over it again and decide where I need to brush up my historical and general knowledge before the start of the tour. Some tour managers take the same tour every time; I prefer to 'mix and match' with tours lasting from three days to two weeks. Mostly the tours are all over Europe, but I sometimes take tours to the US and Canada, and occasionally to the Far East.

The day before my current tour sees me flying to Amsterdam, ready to meet a group flying in from the States for a tour of Europe. I have checked with the Dutch company that is booked to provide the coach, and am told my driver is Erik. Good. I have worked with him before – he has a wonderful sense of humour as long as I don't say anything against his football team, Ajax.

I arrive in the tour hotel the night before, and check room arrangements are OK, then off to bed. I never seem to be able to sleep the night before a tour; I go over and over in my mind potential problem areas. Will clients get on? Will I forget my commentary (a continual nightmare, but why I don't know – as soon as we get near an interesting place the words seem to flow). Next morning I know just how my new group feels as they stumble off the plane with jet lag.

Holding up a company sign, I wait for my group to trickle through Customs. I am double-checking the labels on all the passengers' luggage as they pass, in case anyone misses me. When they are all assembled, I lead the way out to the coach.

As we drive into Amsterdam I welcome them and tell them their programme for the first day. I warn them if they go exploring to watch out for trams; I tell them how many Dutch guilders to the dollar and pass round a card with Dutch money stuck on and the equivalent US amount written on, what we are doing that evening and that if they call the States from their room there will be a charge if they call collect (reverse the charges). I pre-warn them of the times that they will be woken up tomorrow morning, what time they must leave their luggage outside their bedroom doors for the porters to take downstairs to load into the coach (warning them that in Europe we call a bus a coach) and what time breakfast is tomorrow. I also warn them that if they go for a walk to beware of cycles – which have priority on the cycle tracks similar to pedestrian pavements. Funny – each country seems to have its own particular road hazard.

I will repeat tomorrow's timings again this evening, but I need the clients to get into a routine so they feel secure while on tour. I try to book breakfast and other meals at the same time each day. This helps if we have diabetics or others with special feeding needs.

On the way to the hotel we are supposed to give the group a sightseeing tour, but the plane was late and they are all jet-lagged. The hotel said that all the rooms would be ready as the previous group were Japanese who checked out at 6 a.m., so I tell Erik to cut short the tour. Provided we give clients the tour mentioned in their brochure, they are not to know it can last from thirty to ninety minutes – depending on the time we have before hotel rooms are ready.

As I supervise the allocation of room keys, Erik is

unloading the luggage. Most passengers go straight up to their rooms, but one or two wander out to have a look around.

While the passengers sleep off jet-lag, I am checking tomorrow's arrangements: the guide for a tour of Cologne, the Rhine steamer for our hour's trip past the Lorelei Rock, and the hotel. Then there is just time for a trip to C & A – yes, it is a Dutch company founded by Clement and Augustus Brenninkmeyer (hence the initials) to buy some smart white blouses and tops. That is one perk of this job: I buy my shoes and suits in Italy, my tights in France and cosmetics duty free at Geneva Airport.

That evening we have a Welcome meeting, where I go through the itinerary. The hotel is equipped with excellent A/V (audio visual equipment), so instead of giving a speech I give them a slide show – with slides I took last year. Afterwards we take a short walk to the canal-side and board a canal boat for a candlelit dinner as we cruise through Amsterdam's canals. There is an excellent commentary on board (how do the Dutch speak such perfect English?) and the group get to know each other over Dutch beer and cheese. They seem a nice lot; mostly middle-aged, one honeymoon couple and three widows – about par for the course.

Tomorrow we are off to Germany and next evening we will be in Heidelberg. Before I go up to my room I double-check the wake-up calls, the time for breakfast, and that Erik knows when the luggage will be brought down for him to load the coach. Then it is off to my room for a quick look at my notes on German history, before I fall asleep.

Sophie the tour guide

Like Valerie, I check, check and treble-check all the paper-work as soon as it arrives. As soon as I accept a job I ask that the itinerary is faxed through to me; vouchers for entrance fees to local stately homes, lunch, etc. are sent by post.

I need to know where to pick up my clients, where I am to take them, how long is the tour, which is the coach company, how many are in the group, and the name of their tour manager or leader. If I am guiding in another language I need to know which – I guide in three languages: English, French and Italian, but like warning so I can brush up on architectural and other technical terms.

The day before, if there is a lunch booked I phone the restaurant to confirm time of arrival and the menu (so if anyone is vegetarian, diabetic, etc. I can check if they are able to eat what is ordered and change this if necessary before we arrive). That evening I will phone the tour manager at the group's hotel to introduce myself, confirm timings and find out what are the group's interests.

On the day of the tour I always arrive half an hour early, and find the coach driver to discuss the route and check timings. Then into the hotel to find the tour manager and ask if the group are ready to leave.

As the group are milling around, waiting to board the coach, I chat to a few to find out their interests, hobbies and work: it makes a tour more interesting if you can bring in something special for as many of the group as possible. Then it's off, with me setting the scene for the day – where we are going and what we are going to see.

Giving an overview of the history of the area, I point out features as we pass, such as the reason why this town has comparatively wide streets – as it's a market town, traders needed room to set up stalls in the centre of the road.

Passing a Civil War site, I ask the driver to draw into a lay-by while I describe what the scene probably looked like. Then it is on to the county museum with a world-famous collection of fans. I borrow two modern fans from the museum shop, sit a couple of passengers down and teach them and the group the language of fans. Even the men are amused and laugh as I explain how a glance over an open fan was the equivalent of 'come up and see me sometime'.

Of course everyone wants to buy a souvenir fan, but I have allowed time for this. Then it is off to the next stop.

So will you measure up? What skills do you need to carry out Valerie's and Sophie's jobs?

Do you have

- degrees in history, history of art, architecture and diplomacy,
- the patience of Job and the mediating skills of a mother,
- book-keeping experience,
- First Aid qualification,
- excellent stamina,
- fluency in five or more languages,
- a knowledge of food and wine, and
- the ability to read maps accurately

Yes? Well, this is highly unlikely and you could be a dead bore. No? Like everyone else, you work towards obtaining relevant qualifications and honing your skills. You build on your strengths – we all have something to contribute, and it would make for dull guiding if everyone were the same.

A tour manager's job is generally the more complex as tours often go across frontiers. This means that the tour manager has to have a knowledge of the history, economics, history of art and social history of not just one area but several different countries, as well as having more administration to cover.

A guide is regarded as an expert in their area, so will need to have more in-depth knowledge of their subject, and often have a relevant degree.

Some people work solely as tour managers or guides. Others combine both jobs and could work as a local guide one day, and then set off on tour for several days.

The work situation

Although you work as a freelance, you have to become part of the company that employs you, and therefore adopt the company ethos. You need to be adaptable, able to work with a group of teenagers on one tour, and then take charge of a group of OAPs the next.

As you become more experienced you will be able to pick and choose the type of company and clients you work with, but starting out you take every job offered – as long as it is legal.

Sometimes the work involves combinations of different types of work, and this can cause confusion and add to bureaucracy. Tour managers will often cross a country's frontiers; sometimes two or three frontiers in one day. In certain countries only official local guides are allowed to guide visitors, so a tour manager has to be careful they don't infringe the law. Anyone working in the EU should ensure that under the EC Directive 89/48 on Mutual Recognition of Qualifications, they have a professional qualification that is acceptable.

So, along with her passport, Valerie always carries a copy of her diploma, obtained at the end of her training course, which she can show if necessary.

I obtained an OCR (Oxford, Cambridge and RSA) Diploma, and had it translated into the major European languages and certified by the relevant authorities. Other colleagues carry the Tour Managers Certificate issued by IATM (International Association of Tour Managers) or ETOA (European Tour Operators Association).

As I arrive in each new country I have to tell my group about CREST – Currency; Roads; Entertainment; Sightseeing and shopping; Transport and telephones. I can be in the middle of telling the group how to cross the road, or how much to tip taxi drivers and local guides, when I look up and see a policeman's beady eye fastened on me. I dig out my diploma in case he wants to check.

In many areas only locally registered guides are allowed to show visitors around certain sites or buildings. In some countries this is taken to be a whole city. So on your way into Rome or Naples you have to be certain you don't look as if you are doing the job of the local guide. If you are leading your group you cannot guide, or even point out features in Venice, Rome, Florence or other important Italian cities, or guide your group inside Edinburgh Castle, Westminster Abbey or Windsor Castle, unless you have the appropriate qualification.

Rather than making working across borders easier, the EU has devised a Directive to make this more difficult, and it is important that you carry accreditation with you. Valerie can remember when she left her passport at home at the start of a twelve-country tour around Europe, and didn't have one bit of trouble at borders. (Who thought joining the European Community would make it easier to work in Europe!)

On holiday, Valerie took her mother around Windsor Castle one winter morning. The two of them were the only people in the room, and were discussing the paintings. 'As I pointed out a Van Dyck portrait, an attendant came over to say "You know you aren't allowed to guide in here." I thought this was taking things a bit far. But it did emphasize that as tour managers we have to be careful where we give commentaries.'

Freelance work

Ninety-nine per cent of tour managers and guides work as freelances, so need to have some other work to fill in, between seasons. Favourite jobs are working at exhibitions and conferences, field promotions, translating and temporary secretarial work.

When working, once you accept a job, that is binding. You can't accept, and then if a better job comes along ditch the first. There are people who do this, but the word soon gets around and they wonder why they aren't being offered more work. Anyway, it is unethical, and in law a contract, even if it is verbal, is binding.

While we are talking about this . . . you might be approached by one of your company's clients to work directly for them. If you accept, without telling your company, this is unethical and you risk not only losing more work from the company that booked you, but also that as word gets round the other companies they will fight shy of offering you work.

Getting rid of the 'milk run'

Every tourist destination has its milk run. For centuries visitors to Italy have followed a well-travelled path from Venice, through Florence to Rome. Today, in many places visitors to those cities see the backs of the tourists in front of them in queues to see sights. In Britain the traditional route London – Oxford – Chester – Edinburgh – York is so crowded that there is evidence tourists are returning home to warn their friends of the horrors of mass tourism, advising them to avoid the tourist traps.

In order to survive, tour operators will have to offer holidays where visitors get away from their fellow travellers. This needs imagination and commitment, and currently many tour operators prefer to keep on with the milk run as the easy option.

New markets

Once visitors came on 'traditional' tours, staying in one area for days or even weeks. Today time is valuable, and visitors want an 'in-depth' look at an area in a few hours. So you have to be able to précis your information, to be informative and entertaining and provide an appropriate commentary.

Walking, cycling and riding tours are increasing in popularity, as are tours in aid of charities. Managing these is not voluntary work, but interesting work, often off the beaten track.

Case study

On the top floor of New Zealand House, travel journalists were tucking in to a delicious lunch from The Sugar Club and admiring the view, when suddenly they thought they had had too much New Zealand wine. Cycling round the balcony was Cos Kampanaos, dressed in neon-bright lycra. Weaving between the journalists, he was there to announce an innovative cycling holiday in aid of UNICEF.

Cyclists from around the world were being offered the chance of being 'First to the Sun'. Cos said this was an eleven-stage 1,000-kilometre cycling tour along New Zealand's famous Pacific Coast Highway, ending up in Gisborne to be among the first in the world to see the dawn of the new millennium.

Charities are constantly looking for new ways to raise money. Anyone taking part in the 'First to the Sun' ride would not only have to pay for their tour, but also raise funds for the charity. So everyone benefits – New Zealand's tourist industry, the tour operator and their staff who will be handling and looking after the expected 2,000 clients, and the charity.

Similar tours offer clients the chance to run across the Sahara, cycle through Cuba, see the dawn light up Everest – and many, many more. All of these will need tour managers with good administrative ability and a sense of well-organized adventure.

Working conditions

In both jobs, tour managing or guiding, if there is a problem you carry on working until this is sorted out. Valerie says she has lost count of the number of hours she has spent at airports waiting for delayed flights. Sophie says luckily she doesn't have as many delays as Valerie, but if a client has to be taken to hospital she will accompany them, and stay translating until friends or colleagues arrive.

Clients can get very irate, but Valerie and Sophie both say 'Try to remember they are shouting because they feel they have been let down on their holiday, rather than by you.'

Some companies provide a uniform, and however awful you think this is, it saves money as this type of work plays havoc with clothes.

Hours can be long, and you must have good stamina. As a freelance you don't get paid if you are ill, so budget for medical insurance so you can choose when you go into hospital for treatment. Being self-employed, you are responsible for your own National Insurance and income tax (a good accountant is extremely useful). Don't think that if you are paid cash you don't have to declare earnings. Companies have to account for every penny they disburse, and eventually their countries' computers will connect up with your Inland Revenue office, and you could be caught for unpaid tax years later.

Will you enjoy the work? Yes, if you

- like people,
- enjoy doing research,
- have an insatiable curiosity about the world around you, and what makes people tick,
- are organized and able to work on your own,
- are not afraid of phoning and phoning companies to find work,
- dress smartly,
- are aged between 16 and 75,
- have lots of stamina, and
- have a clear speaking voice.

Strange – but true

Some very good people working in this sector are shy. But 'hiding behind their knowledge', they are able to enthuse clients with their love of their job.

There is work for people who want to look after visitors at museums, galleries, stately homes, in national parks, etc. These can be called guides, interpreters, wardens, etc. Often they don't have formal training, but have fallen into the job by chance. Others may be very experienced professional people such as architects, ex-Services personnel, musicians, actors, designers, etc. who are employed because of their in-depth knowledge to run special tours.

Case study

As head of Scotland Yard's Diplomatic Protection branch, Allen Evershed was in charge of 500 policemen. He gained a fascinating insight into London's embassies and their history, and was often in charge of VIP visits where he got to know people 'behind the scenes'.

When it was time to retire, he wanted to do something to show others the fascinating world of unknown London. He decided he needed to gain guiding skills, so as a start took a short course for the OCR (Oxford, Cambridge and RSA) Certificate. Using information on the course on tapping potential markets, he started his own company to show couples and small groups 'behind the scenes' of his old patch.

2 Tour managers

As a group travels from one region or country to another, they need someone to handle the administration of the tour, i.e. the tour manager – also known as tour leader, tour administrator, tour director, tour guide or courier. Their knowledge, diplomatic and linguistic skills and stamina are essential to make sure touring holidays come up to clients' expectations.

Working as a tour manager generally means travelling with your group and being away from your base at night.

The IATM (International Association of Tour Managers) says a tour manager is someone who

- manages and supervises the itinerary on behalf of the tour operator, ensuring the programme is carried out as described in the tour operator's literature and sold to the traveller consumer
- furnishes background information en route, covering general and particular ethnic, geographic, historic and socio-economic aspects of the country visited as well as local practical information

Usually clients travel by coach, but transport can be by train, with Eurostar part of many European tours, private limousine or even plane – or a combination of these. An increasingly popular option is riding, walking or cycling tours, but these are very different from the old idea of cheap and cheerful tourism. Instead of backpacks and hostels, today's groups have their luggage transported for them between top-class hotels.

Once, Valerie and her colleagues were just thrown in at the deep end, and sank or swam after their first trip. Usually they sank without trace, vowing never to get back on a coach again, let alone in charge of a group. A few, like Valerie, survived the experience, and went on to lead tours all over the world.

What the work entails

Tour managing is work 'on the move' when you accompany visitors on short breaks or longer tours, either in your home country or abroad. Working 'on the move' generally means working on a coach. So you can't suffer from motion sickness. The work involves being away from your base at night, travelling with your group.

Some jobs

Coach tour guide (sometimes known as courier)

This is *not* an official job title, but used by many companies to describe staff who are generally in their first or second year of working for a coach company or tour operator. Looking after groups for short breaks, and sometimes longer tours, usually on coaches. The job involves basic tour administration, supervising seating, check-ins at accommodation, checking luggage onto the coach after each overnight stop, giving a basic commentary, arranging stops, helping solve problems, etc.

Tour manager

An experienced tour guide who has worked several seasons in the industry, and is responsible for administration of the tour, with an in-depth knowledge of the history, geography, culture, food and economics of tour countries. Tour managers usually speak several languages. After two or three years' experience, they can apply to become a member of IATM (International Association of Tour Managers).

Tour director

In Europe this can mean the same job as a senior tour manager. In America this often means a tour leader, sometimes with student groups.

Conference/incentive conference tour manager

Many conferences offer pre- and post-conference tours that need tour managers to accompany them. Staff may need to have some specialist knowledge, or know how to obtain this. For example, post-medical-conference tours could cover visits to well-known hospitals, and the tour manager would need to know where to find the hospitals, confirm arrangements for specialist lectures etc. as well as organizing tour administration, and be able to give a commentary on history and sites en route.

Incentive conferences often need people with social skills as well as good basic administration, to accompany guests, often travelling abroad.

It is said that every man has two countries: his own and France, and this country is probably the most popular in the world as a conference and incentive conference destination.

Case study

Mary Minzly runs Spectra Continental France, a top destination management company. She devises tailor-made programmes for some of the world's most prestigious companies. 'We plan and operate incentive travel programmes, meetings of every shape and size, as well as high-calibre special interest programmes throughout France.'

Always looking for new ideas 'to make programmes exceptional and memorable experiences', her company will employ freelance staff to assist in looking after clients as they are taken to the US Cemetery at Omaha, visit the Chateau de Chenonceau, take part in a wine-tasting at Clos Vougeot (sorry, you will be much too busy to take part!), eat a dinner cooked by Paul Bocuse and his brigade, and be greeted by the Garde Républicaine when attending the Paris Opéra.

This type of work demands staff who are very smart, speak languages fluently and are prepared to work all hours if a problem arises. In return you have the chance to participate in their fabulous programmes and experience events that normally you would only read about.

Adventure tour and sports guide

Companies that offer adventure tours need staff who have the right sports qualifications and First Aid, and are also good leaders.

Walking, cycling and riding tours

Once these tours were for hardy backpackers. Today it is chic to wander in a group through off-the-beaten-track Tuscany or Spain. Up-market companies generally employ two staff: a guide/leader and a tour manager. Companies look for staff who can empathize with the special type of person who goes on these tours.

Case history

Sam

The day before a VIP group is due to arrive, Sam, a small tour operator offering specialized tours, is phoned by Theo, the freelance tour manager he has booked to look after a group. Theo has been booked for months to look after this group, but has glandular fever. Panic.

'I need to replace Theo – impossible – before 7.30 tomorrow morning. I start phoning. In this day and age it is incredible how many tour managers don't have answering machines – or if they have, haven't updated them. By the time I get on to my "third priority" list, a good hour has gone by. Hurrah – someone is there. Ask Helen is she free? No – but what was the job? If she can't do the job, why waste my time asking? Makes me think she is on the third list because obviously unreliable; asking with a view to cancelling her current job if I come up with a better one.

'It is now lunch time and some people are arriving home; but what time-wasters. They are incapable of saying no, without a lot of chat. I cut them off – knowing I am getting a reputation for rudeness. Others take great delight in telling me they have been booked for months. Fine, I booked Theo months ago too, but things do happen. Finally, I get on to my "impossible" list and dial Sue. I never contact her because she is so good she is always booked up. Her answering machine says she will be back the next day – and is free for six days (my tour is five). It even gives a telephone number where I can contact her in Paris. Phoning her, she says she is free, but can't get to Heathrow before 9.30. I arrange to meet her at the airport with her paperwork and I will meet the client, explain about Theo and hope he realizes he is very, very lucky to get Sue. So am I. Phew!'

A day in Sue's life
'Poor Sam sounded almost suicidal when he phoned me. But having met his client, Monsieur Le Blanc, I can understand why. He owns one of the most exclusive travel agencies in San Diego, and hovers around, twittering and getting in everyone's way.

'We meet up at Heathrow and I find difficulty getting Sam to one side to ask about the float and what this would cover – telephone calls, porterage, road tolls (usually the driver pays – but not with all companies), can I order champagne if anyone has an anniversary or birthday? I have to do something about this, so tactfully bolster Le Blanc's ego by asking if he would like to ensure his clients are seated in the right seats in the coach (having made sure that all my goods and chattels are dumped on the front seat with no chance of moving them – and the driver primed to ensure I have both seats free; you don't want someone asking questions while you are looking for the next place to talk about, while keeping an eye on the map if the route is new to the driver).

'I get my paperwork from Sam, and am pleased to discover that at least there are no money worries as he hands over a huge wad of travellers' cheques for the float. When I see the hotel list I understand why. This is going to be fun, and a change from the usual "three-star" tourist hotels I have to contend with. We are lunching at Wren's Old House Hotel in Windsor, and spending a quiet afternoon ambling around Eton and Windsor. Then it's off to Waterloo for a late afternoon departure on Eurostar to Paris. First night is in the Crillon, one of the best hotels in the world, and after that it is quality all the way with stays in Relais et Chateau hotels (a top hotel marketing consortium with the highest standards).

'The group have interests in electronics, and we are ending our short trip in Eindhoven, Dutch home to the giant Philips corporation, and staying at the Collse Hoeve Hotel. The hotel's theme is rocking-horses – hope the group have a sense of humour. If so they will love the horses, especially the ones in the bathrooms.

'During lunch I go through the paperwork and see I must confirm the final gala dinner at Evoluon, Eindhoven's incredible futuristic dome where the catering is by the Roux brothers.

'It will be a wonderful experience to take this group, but travellers with this amount of money can sometimes be a pain – or a delight. Luckily for me they are the latter, and once Monsieur Le Blanc realizes I do know my job, and even better that I have made a study of Huguenot history (he is proud of being one), we get on fine. I make a mental note to look up the route taken by many Huguenot refugees; when they were kicked out of France many went to the Netherlands, and then on to England, and would have taken the same route that we are following three hundred years later.

'I suggest to everyone that we have a "quiet hour" after lunch every day; as we drive along they sleep off lunch and I can catch up with paperwork. With this type of group everything has to be planned meticulously; they are used to running large companies and don't expect anything to go wrong.

'So it is check, check and check again, with my mobile phone going non-stop. Luckily the astronomical phone costs will be covered by the float.

'Five days later, I wave goodbye at Amsterdam Airport
to a group who have become friends. Sam — any time you
want a tour manager . . .!'

Luxury rambles

Walking tours also need tour managers. No longer do ramblers
have to carry their tents on their walk. Today, the party sets off
in the morning, leaving their suitcases to be transported to their
next luxury hotel on the itinerary, while they set off to see an
unexplored part of Spain, Italy or another beautiful country.
Their tour manager is there to help the guide with the tour
administration as they ramble through old villages and vineyards.

Alternative Travel is probably the doyen of this type of
company, and selects their tour managers very carefully. In fact,
they have two staff with every tour of sixteen clients: one is the
leader who accompanies the group from place to place, and has
to abide by their 'two-minute' rule — you give a talk or describe
something in two minutes, so clients aren't bored. Each group
has a tour manager, who drives the support mini-coach, buys and
sets up the superb picnics and carries out the tour administration.

If this sounds like your type of work, Alternative Travel
suggest you send two first-class stamps for a brochure (these are
works of art, designed to attract a very special connoisseur-type
of client). Study the tours, and if you are interested apply to the
company.

If selected, you will be sent on a training course where you
learn things such as always carrying small plastic bags. Why? So
you can give these out to smoker clients to put their cigarette
butts in — so they don't leave any litter.

The luggage transport is usually a small coach which meets
the group at a pre-arranged lunch spot. The tour manager has
to have enough basic cooking and presentation skills to set up
the picnics, described by grateful clients as 'works of art', so that
when they arrive there is the delicious lunch of local specialities
already set up. After lunch, if anyone feels tired, they go off in
the coach with the tour manager to the next hotel, while the
guide/leader takes the rest off for another ramble.

So this type of company will employ tour managers with a love of food!

Setting up your own company

There is work for those who want to start on their own. Many people, especially those with specialist knowledge such as architects, ex-wine trade staff etc., set up their own companies offering specialized tours.

N.B. If you want to work in Europe, under the EC Directive 89/48, Mutual Recognition of Qualifications, it is advisable to have a qualification accepted in the EU and carry this with you at all times. According to reports in *On the Road* and *Coaching Monthly*, Continental police are now asking for evidence of qualification, particularly in France, Portugal, Austria and Italy.

Training

Previously, tour managers had little or no training in looking after groups, but today the majority start by taking a course. IATM have had input to the course run at Breda in the Netherlands. In Britain there is a distance learning course run by Leisure World for the basics, and you can then take a practical week leading to an OCR qualification.

Once you have taken a basic course, you will find any extra qualifications, such as a degree in history, history of art, architecture, etc., extremely useful.

More and more companies are insisting on a current First Aid course.

For more details about training, see Chapter 5.

Working conditions

You can't suffer from travel sickness, and will need to have reserves of stamina, as days can be very long.

The law says that a driver has to have a day off; there is no such law for tour managers, and however long the tour, those are the days you work. If someone is ill this can involve you working through the night to get them to hospital and make arrangements, then returning to the hotel ready to move on with the group to the next country – and no chance of even five minutes' rest. You become an expert at stepping into the shower fully clothed, to save time washing yourself and your clothes.

You have to be self-sufficient. Generally, for a successful tour you have to keep a certain distance from passengers, while being a friend to all – a difficult combination.

You and the driver work as a team. He (or she) is your ally, friend and workmate. It helps if you like football (or can feign an interest in the most important feature of most Continental and British drivers' lives).

You sit with the driver during meals; if you sit with passengers, human nature in the others may object to what is seen as favouritism toward the people you sit between. Although you feel you are doing your duty, to others it can cause resentment. When with clients you are always on duty, so if you don't have an hour or two away from tour problems, you become stale.

If you take tours by train or plane, these can be very lonely. You are in charge of the group going from one place to another, with no coach driver to talk to.

Warning! Luggage is the bane of your life. Generally you are in charge, and if a piece goes missing it's down to you to sort out the problem. You can always tell tour managers off duty: they are the ones automatically counting each pile of luggage outside an hotel or at the airport.

3 Guides

The dictionary defines a guide as someone who points out the way; who leads others on a trip or tour; and one who directs, or serves as the model for, another in his conduct, career, etc.

The CEN Working Group (a European committee for standardization) defines a tourist guide as the person who guides visitors in the language of their choice and interprets the cultural and natural heritage of an area, which person may possess an area-specific qualification. Such qualifications exist in EU countries. They are usually issued and/or recognized by the appropriate authority.

Generally a guide will work in one area or city, returning home at night. They must be mature in outlook, with good health.

Guides are employed to

- look after visitors to an area,
- accompany visitors on day tours to different venues, and
- look after visitors to museums, factories, galleries, national parks, gardens, etc.

The BBC TV programme *Tourist Trouble* sent shock waves through the industry. Sadly it emphasized all the worst aspects of group travel – from visitors being shouted at to 'follow me', to the coach driver politely ticking off the guide for not being at the meeting point (a touch of drivers getting their own back on guides who just don't keep to time).

Colleagues of the people featured were horrified at the way they were portrayed – but perhaps the programme highlighted what might be changed in guiding and training for Britain.

When it is repeated, watch carefully and make sure you aren't copying the bad points highlighted.

Tourist boards say the role and function of a guide is to organize, inform and entertain. The work is rewarding, with opportunities to meet a wide range of people, to travel and to manage your own working environment. Guides in the UK are mainly freelance, and self-employed. Work is seasonal, involving unsociable hours, and usually obtained by direct contact with tour operators and other agencies, so you must be self-sufficient and able to market yourself.

Companies look for maturity, an outgoing personality, smart appearance, physical stamina, good general knowledge, organizational ability, flexibility, a genuine interest in people and the motivation to develop your own business.

Different jobs

There are innumerable jobs working for tour operators, coach operators, city, town or regional authorities; heritage sites; factories open to the public; distilleries, vineyards, wine houses, historic houses, castles, cathedrals and important churches; conference and incentive conference organizers; government agencies; hall porters; museums, galleries, hotels, national parks; cycling-, walking-, adventure- and horse-riding-tour operators; student tour companies, guided tour companies, specialized tour operators; farms, schools, industrial heritage centres, associations, gardens; to a small extent regional and local tourist boards, and any company or venue that needs someone to look after visitors and show them around.

Some examples of guiding jobs are:

In-house guides
Working in stately homes, historic houses, castles, cathedrals and important churches, factories open to the public, distilleries, wine houses, farms, galleries, and other tourist venues. Jobs are generally part-time.

Once these jobs were usually voluntary, but as the tourism industry becomes more professional, venues increasingly pay their guides. Even the National Trust has had to acknowledge that around Wimbledon time it is extremely difficult to find voluntary staff.

Registered guide

This is a guide who has followed a training course and taken an examination administered by a tourist board. Often guides' names are published in official regional tourist board literature which helps with finding jobs, and in some towns or areas only registered guides are allowed in certain historic buildings (e.g. Windsor Castle, the Tower of London, Westminster Abbey, Edinburgh Castle). In Britain guides are often known as 'Blue Badges' from the badge colour. There are also 'Green Badges' which denote a regional guide in certain areas.

Sophie's day

Sophie is a registered guide, working in one of England's beautiful cathedral cities. She is often booked to guide visiting groups staying in her area.

'My day actually starts the night before, when I phone the tour leader of next day's group at their hotel. Introducing myself, I confirm the meeting time and where we are to go, then ask if the group wants to see anything special. Usually this is just a courtesy call, but it reassures the tour leader that I will actually turn up, and prevents surprises – so I'm not faced with "we want to see so-and-so" when I only have the haziest knowledge of an obscure site. It also gives me time to look it up in my card file index or local guide books.

'Half an hour before departure I am in the hotel, asking the receptionist where I can find the coach driver. He is having breakfast, after cleaning and washing his coach. Smartly dressed, Mark seems very professional and we start to plan the day together. He admits he knows the area well (that will help me so I can concentrate on my talk, rather than having to direct the driver), so we discuss the route while Mark tells me of any special items he thinks passengers will want mentioned. The tour leader is a young university student, Dennis, who joins us – and it is obvious that although he is new he works hard and is keen to learn.

'I get very annoyed with some colleagues who decry youngsters starting out in this profession. We all had to start somewhere, yet the moment some guides get their "blue badge" they think they know it all and are vastly superior. I seldom wear my badge – can never find it and everyone knows me – and it makes me laugh the way some guides turn their noses up if I join their table for coffee; implying because I don't wear a badge I am an amateur.

'Dennis gets his group onto the coach, introduces me – and off we go. They come from the States, and I hear interested murmurs as I mention some of the Pilgrim Fathers who came from this area, and point out their homes. History comes alive when you can relate to incidents. As we go into a church containing the impressive tomb of the family who founded their State capital city, they are all chattering and obviously enjoying the day. I have told them they can take photos in this church, but ask that photographers drop a contribution into the box as we leave.

'Then it is on to coffee, and the all-important "comfort stop". I never let passengers use the coach loo – easiest way to spread tummy bugs, however clean a driver keeps it. Drivers often hang a sign saying "out of order", or I say that the door springs open so I have locked it, but "if anyone wants to use the loo to let me know" – they never bother.

'Gently poking fun at British eccentricity as we pass a cricket match, I ask Mark to pull in while I give them a five-minute round-up of the rules – when your team is *out* you are *in*, etc. It is wonderful to have them laughing at me, and when we stop for coffee one comes up to tell me "Gee Sophie, I can't understand a word of what you say but I love your cute accent."

'On the way to lunch we pass through marvellous woods, which give me the cue to tell them the meaning of sayings such as "by hook or by crook". In the old days peasants were allowed to go into their Lord's woods and gather wood for fuel, using their work tools: shepherds crooks and bill hooks. The group like this, so I tell them more (which I found in the *Tourism English Dictionary*). "Little bits" always go down well.

'History? Yes, of course. I am paid to give visitors an insight into my area, and I tailor my talk to the audience. However, they are much more interested if I talk about life in Tudor times and say that people had a bath once a year – then go into social history of the period. Rather than give them lots of dates of people of whom they have never heard.

'That afternoon we are visiting a stately home, which gives me a chance to catch up on paperwork while the house guides take over. The group will come out via the café, so I sit there with a free cup of tea and delicious home-made scone (perks of the job) while I write out my invoice for today's work. Dennis has given me the tour operator's voucher (they won't pay me without this), and as I stroll across the road to post the invoice I reflect that operators tell me they despair of guides who send in invoices days or even weeks after a job, delaying their own and other payments.

'On the way back we go through some attractive villages, and as Mark will be driving slowly through these I take the time to walk back down the coach and answer questions (holding on tightly as we go). I don't believe in talking too much; rather I prefer to set the scene and then let visitors say "there's one of those things Sophie told us about". Talking face to face also helps visitors to ask questions about life here; sometimes I am the only local they get to meet.

'It is lovely when "my" group gets off the coach thanking me for an enjoyable day. What other job gives you constant praise? Then it is home to confirm the next day's tour . . .'

Boat and open-top bus guides

Although the major sightseeing boat operators now have massive 'ships' with recorded commentaries, luckily for humans the technology is too expensive for smaller operators, so there is still work in major river cities. If you are serious about your work, take a trip on a Parisian *Bateau Mouche* – the guided commentary soon shows you how important it is to point out sights – people crane to see the buildings mentioned – as there isn't enough time to identify how to recognize them. Many major tourist cities now have open-topped bus tours, again needing guides.

Site guides
At monumental sites, guides can work in the open air for local authorities, heritage sites, archaeological digs, etc. Other work may be found in museums, factories, craft workshops, etc.

For years visitors wanted to go inside Buckingham Palace – and suddenly the Queen opened her doors to visitors. You would imagine the Palace would be one of the top attractions, yet *Holiday Which?* says it scores lowest marks for quality as an attraction. Their site guides or attendants only have four days training, so visitors are often frustrated that they can't get information when they ask about pictures or furniture.

The Palace suggest visitors buy the guide book (more expense); high on historical information but short on anecdotes. 'Little effort is made to bring state rooms to life.' The same survey also highlighted the way visitors felt they were being 'processed' through.

However, some sites have excellent guides. The *Holiday Which?* survey highlighted the 'Beefeaters' tours of the Tower of London, which are rated 'the best part of the visit'. The yeomen warders, or 'Beefeaters' live in the Tower, and are part of the living history of the site, with funds of interesting anecdotes that bring the Tower's story to life.

The *Holiday Which?* survey was interesting because it questioned the British public, who make up a large proportion of tourist visitors, rather than just overseas visitors. It is as well to remember that the major growth in guided tours comes from weekend breaks for British tourists, rather than the traditional 'milk run' tours for foreign visitors around Britain, which are on the decline.

Trail guide

National parks, the Forestry Commission, etc. need people who are wildlife enthusiasts, understanding the countryside and wanting to show it off to visitors. There are more and more guided walks being organized, showing off everything from birds and other wildlife to mushrooming, and suchlike.

Similarly, cycling, walking and riding tour operators need guides that are energetic and able to accompany individual visitors through the countryside on walking or cycling tours for a certain section or day. These holidays are split between 'managed' tours (see Chapter 2) and individual clients who 'go it alone', having their hotels booked and luggage transported in-between, but look after themselves during the day. Sometimes these individuals will have a guided tour for a special sector or day.

In this area guided walks often develop as part of a job. English Nature have reserves across England, and to encourage visitors and understanding of their conservation role, site managers organize and lead an excellent programme of guided walks, covering interests from orchids to seal-watching. Training for this type of guiding is very much 'on the job'. If your group starts dropping off you soon learn to tailor your enthusiasm to their walking capabilities.

Walking-tour guide

Walking tours, of an area, village, town, city or cemetery, are the fastest-expanding sector for half-day tours.

N.B. Some walking-tour guides work for companies that advertise the tours. Guides turn up at the advertised meeting place, and collect the tour fee, usually taking a percentage of this fee. You are paid per person; even if only one client turns up, you are still expected to take them on the full tour.

The Original London Walks are probably the oldest tour operators in this field, and their programme proves just what can be offered to tempt visitors. Who could resist Alan (the one with the dark hat and green carnation) who takes you to see 'Spies' and Spycatchers' London'? Or Stephanie taking you around to see 'How the Other Half Lives'? There are walks offering 'Classic Murders and Crimes'. 'Haunted Pubs' (a winner anywhere) and 'Canal Walks' led by Roger, who is an expert canoeist.

Living in a beautiful old town, popular as a weekend destination for visitors, Sophie thought when she first qualified she would start by offering guided walks. Talking this over with her tutor on her guide training course, the tutor suggested she make friends with local hall porters in the big hotels and ask if they would be interested in offering tours as a service for guests.

So one afternoon she went to talk to hall porters and explained that she was interested in taking hotel guests around – perhaps before or after dinner for short tours. Bernie at the Grand Hotel was particularly interested, and took Sophie's telephone number. 'We often get overseas clients who want something to do, and are bored just sitting in the lounge,' he told her.

Now Sophie offers walking tours of her city in the winter to visiting clients who want to get out and look around. She has printed 'flyers' (small leaflets) which Bernie displays on his desk. He takes the bookings, and he and Sophie split the fee. There are so many demands for tours that Sophie now shares the work with two colleagues, and is thinking of setting up her own company to offer tours on a more regular basis, and tap into the conference tours market.

In the New Forest, the visitor centre organizes guided walks. Raymond Stickland, as a 'commoner', is allowed to let his beef cattle graze on the grassland, and he also helps look after visitors by taking them on fascinating guided tours. Ray showed us deer – which I loved; and snakes – which I didn't. Male deer are the ones with the antlers, which they shed each year, and Ray explained about the rutting season, named different types of deer, and pointed out mushrooms, telling us which ones we could eat, and which ones were poisonous.

Then we met up with his friend Dave Hellyer, another guide, who pointed out 'chicken in the wood' mushrooms which do taste of chicken. He also knows where you can see badgers on a night watch, and this is very popular with visitors. A special observation room has been built with a one-way glass wall

looking onto a badger sett, and at night visitors can see the
badgers coming and going – they are nocturnal creatures. The
glass has one advantage: it keeps the smell out!

Jane Paterson comes from a famous London guiding family;
both her husband and her daughter Pattie work as guides. Jane
is also a qualified guide for the Houses of Parliament, and takes
visitors around on tours of these world-famous buildings. Most
people are suitably impressed and enjoy their visit to see
something that normally they would only see on TV. However,
there are problems: 'French school children,' sighs Jane. 'They
come in because it is the cheapest tour option, but the teachers
haven't been into their Parliament buildings in their own
country.'

Guided tours have to fit in with Parliament's administrative
structure. It has been in place for hundreds of years, and guides
have to be sympathetic to this, even though it might cause
problems for tour administration.

Interpreter

These are not language speakers, but people who 'interpret' or
explain the background and history of industrial heritage sites,
some stately homes, castles, mines, etc. Venues need staff to
'interpret' manufacturing processes, how people lived, etc., and
anyone who has worked in industry is often welcomed for their
specialized knowledge. For example, some mines that have
closed down are being opened up to visitors, who are taken
around by ex-miners.

Some sites expect guides to wear costume, and it can help if
you like amateur dramatics. Museums such as Beamish Open
Air Museum in Northumberland and the Ironbridge Gorge
Museum in Shropshire have turned these jobs into a fascinating
part of any visit to their sites. At Beamish one guide cooks barley
sugar sweets, explains how these sweets were made in the old
days, then sells them to eager customers. At Ironbridge they
show off candle-making, and visitors learn that 'burning the
candle at both ends' came from the days when poor people
would bend in half a cheap candle made of rushes, put it in a
holder and burn both ends to give double the light.

Case study

If it hadn't been for a chronic shortage of money (usual student problem) you would never have found Tom done up in his sister's tights and a 'Tudor' outfit. Studying history at university, Tom saw a notice asking for people to act as guides at the local stately home. 'Just the job,' thought Tom, especially keen to put his historical knowledge to good use. Then he saw 'Guides will be expected to wear Tudor costume'. 'That's good-bye to that idea,' he thought.

Next morning the post produced not one, but three bills, which helped Tom make up his mind that perhaps becoming a guide wasn't such a bad option. After a short interview he was given a script to learn and a costume to wear. Expecting a training course, he turned up the next day and was told to get into his costume immediately: 'one of the guides is ill and there is a group of Americans arriving in thirty minutes'.

Being thrown in at the deep end didn't give Tom any time to get embarrassed. Thank heavens he had studied the script for hours last night. When the group arrived he found they were college kids, luckily pretty bored with 'all this history', so Tom started to tell them that the Tudors would only have had a bath once a year. This went down very well. Tom soon realized that he had been talking for an hour, and the group leader was thanking him and saying they had to leave. But not before all the prettiest girls had lined up to have their photo taken with him.

His historical knowledge means Tom can vary tours to suit different groups, and he has become used to his outfit – well, almost. He likes the guiding part of his job, and when term starts again he is going to look into the possibilities of taking a guide course so he can progress onwards.

One venue that makes full use of guides in historical dress is the Shrewsbury Quest. Guides' outfits are habits as would have been worn by a twelfth-century monk, following the theme set by the *Brother Cadfael* TV series. Ellis Peters' medieval crime novels have dramatically increased visitors to this attractive Shropshire town, and the guides really 'live' their roles in the reconstructed buildings depicting life at the Abbey in Cadfael's time. A recent article in the *Daily Telegraph* told of one visitor who was heard telling a guide 'I think it's a real credit to you; a young lad like you giving up normal life.'

Farm tourism

'Townies' are keen to know about the countryside, so more and more opportunities arise looking after visitors who visit farms, go on nature walks, etc.

Longdown Dairy in the New Forest is one of this type of farm, which is commercially viable because of farm tourism. 'Townies', especially children, love to see animals and pet them. As visitors arrive, Pippin the Border Collie and Monty the Jack Russell meet them at the gate, and to the delight of children, escort them around the farm, aided by farm manager Catherine Bint.

Catherine is a 'natural' guide; her fascinating talks have taken a lot of work to deliver and produce information tailored to visitors' needs. She talks about life on a farm, tailoring her talk to town children who think milk begins life in Tetra Paks, or to visiting farmers wanting to discuss crop yields. Children love watching the cows being milked, and putting their hands inside a wooden model to find out how they give birth – no gooseberry bushes here! Then Christine takes them on to the rabbit den, where they sit among the animals, able to pick them up and cuddle them under supervision.

Ski guide

In Alpine countries this means a fully qualified person able to take visitors skiing on different runs. Some British chalet operators advertise that their staff show visitors around, and try to get round the regulations by calling these staff 'hosts'. In France, especially, 'guides' cannot operate unless they have taken stringent official French tests, and recently British staff who have fallen foul of French regulations have found themselves behind bars.

Ski guides have to take an intensive course, open to British participants as long as they satisfy the authorities and speak the local language. Although British qualifications may soon be acceptable in the Alps, one of the reasons given by the French in particular not to recognize these is the lack of local weather knowledge. If you are going to have people's lives in your hands, you owe it to them to take a local course to learn how to read weather conditions.

Some resorts now offer guided walking tours on snowshoes.

Conference work
Many conferences offer half- and full-day tours to interest people who are accompanying delegates, but not taking part in the conference. There is also work for pre- and post-conference tours, generally organized to give delegates a part-holiday and part-study tour.

A typical day on a conference programme; or, less is best

Sophie meets the coach on the way to the Manor Hotel. She wants to cast an eye over the interior to see that head-rest covers are all in place, the driver's uniform is smart, and there are no dirty ashtrays. When the coach arrives she sees Dave is the driver, so she knows that everything will be spotless; she and Dave work well as a team and the clients should have a good day.

Arriving early at the Manor Hotel, over a cup of coffee they run through the programme and she reminds Dave that at their first stop, a local stately home, the guests are specially invited as normally it isn't open to the public. Lady Harton will be waiting to greet the group, and Dave has to drive through the rather narrow gates and park right in front of the house. Luckily Dave has been there before and says there is plenty of room for the coach to get through the gates – at least an inch on each side!

The group are 'accompanying persons' – all wives – at a medical conference. While their husbands are participating in a live hook-up with a local general hospital where a world-famous surgeon is demonstrating a new operation, the wives are settling into the coach prepared to enjoy their day as guests of the British (albeit some very aristocratic Britishers!).

Guiding a conference group is different from a 'normal' tour. The guests are all well-travelled, and welcome the chance to meet up with old friends. Sophie gives an introduction to set the scene for the day, and then turns off the mike to give everyone a chance to catch up on gossip. Definitely in these circumstances, although you must ensure that guests enjoy their day, as far as commentaries go – less is usually best!

As they arrive at the stately home, Lady Harton is on the steps to meet the group, and gives them coffee and home-made biscuits before taking them on a tour showing off what she calls her disreputable ancestors, and soon has the group eating out of her hand.

Then it's off to lunch at another private house which is never open to the public. The owner sometimes gives groups lunch, and as they file into the dining room there is a gasp as they see a huge table laid out with sparkling crystal and silver plates at each place. Sophie has to tell the guests seated either side of her that it is perfectly all right to wipe their fingers on the exquisite lace napkins. She is very proud as she feels it is nice to show that we still have some wonderful treasures left in Britain; not everything has been sold abroad.

By this time most of the group are sleepy after two visits and a grand lunch, so they are happy to make their way down the garden path to the river running through the grounds, where a narrow boat is waiting to take them on a leisurely trip downstream to where Dave and the coach is waiting for them. The scenery is lovely, but most of the group nod off.

Conference tours are the icing on the cake, and Sophie has made a hit with the organizer, who whispers to her, when she returns with her happy group, to phone her as she has lots more work for her with a series of conferences she has just been asked to organize.

Guest lecturer

Although technically a different job, many tour managers and guides with specialist knowledge are asked to join tours and cruises to give clients an in-depth tour. This can seem a delightful assignment: one is being paid to visit a part of the world in which one has an enduring interest. But then, according to ex-ambassador Sir John Ure, 'The jokers in the pack begin to come out.' Panic sets in early. In the departure lounge at Heathrow, no fewer than four passengers have noses buried deeply into the very book on which one has based a lecture; what hope has one of informing – let alone impressing – them?

The cruise director says 'I'm sure you'll wow them, Sir John', and mentions that his slot is between the conjuror and the Filipino dancers. Woe betide you if there is a crisis on Wall Street, and passengers are on their mobile phones rather than listening to you.

One of the most popular companies employing guest lecturers is Swan Hellenic, offering cruises with an unlimited variety of topics. Travellers on its cruises tend to be well informed and interested in every aspect of where they are going. But it can happen that travellers have actually written the books you use for research – so it's back to the research library to find something new.

Antiques courier

You have to have an in-depth knowledge of antiques. Clients contact you and say they are interested in purchasing certain antiques. You work out an itinerary setting up appointments and visits to antique dealers who specialize in the appropriate pieces. Generally you meet clients at an airport, drive them around in your car, and probably arrange their accommodation. You will have to take out 'hire and reward' car insurance, which can be expensive.

Step-on guide

This is a descriptive American term for a guide who meets a touring group, 'steps on' the coach for a tour of their area, then leaves the coach as the tour continues on to the next stop.

Press officer

They may not think of themselves as guides, but by virtue of their work any press officer of a tourist board has to guide their region. Because they have to liaise with their journalist guests, and show and talk about what interests writers, they think about what their visitor wants to know, and react accordingly.

Many crafts and industries also have press officers who need to know their history, and how to guide journalists around. As press officer for the Scotch Whisky Association, Campbell Evans is often seen on television, talking about his industry. But he is also a fantastic guide. It is his job to take visitors around who are going to promote whisky; on a recent visit to Speyside he talked knowledgeably about the history and characteristics of distilleries, and even showed some smugglers' tools. Fascinating!

Work tip

If you live near Speyside, it may be useful to know that many distilleries employ guides in the summer.

Working conditions

Unless employers offer training on site, it is essential to take a course first; even if it is just a basic course in customer care and delivering commentaries. For your own benefit, however much you are convinced you can handle a visiting group, you should know that the most erudite and fluent speaker dries up if they haven't been taught how to deliver a commentary on a microphone on a moving coach, or how to keep a group interested who are walking around behind you.

Each job will involve research, tailoring your commentary to clients. Just because you have taken a course, or completed in-house training, doesn't mean that you learn the commentary off parrot-fashion and deliver the same talk to every visitor. Unless you want to become that type of boring guide who switches on their tape-recorder mind at the beginning of the day, and switches off at night.

These guides are the bane of Jim's life. Driving coaches around London, he says 'These metronome guides bore me rigid

– so what do they do to passengers? It is great fun to play a game with them. I'll tell them the usual route is blocked and dive down a side street. You should see the panic in their eyes when they don't know where they are, because they have never bothered to see what goes on either side of their blinkered noses.'

So don't become a 'metronome guide'.

4 Planning your working day

It would be a dull world if we were all the same, and every tour manager and guide will have their own way of working. Valerie and Sophie give pointers to the way they organize their work and what can be involved.

Check documentation the moment it arrives

- Times and dates.
- Name of coach company.
- Pick-up point – and for tours, list of hotels.
- Name of group.
- Number of clients.
- Nationality/special interests/special instructions.
- Any problem areas.
- Entrances and visits – where and who pays.

Day/evening before

- Phone any group leader and coach company to confirm details.

Start

- Arrive early.
- Confirm route and stops with the coach driver.
- Test the mike and clean with an antiseptic wipe.
- If the coach has a legal courier seat, test the belt. If it doesn't have this seat, or a belt, reserve a pair of front seats for yourself (it is distracting having someone sitting next to you, and others in the group get jealous).

When clients arrive

- Smile a greeting. They are just as anxious as you.
- Sort out seating.
- If starting a tour, ensure each client has seen their luggage being placed in the boot.
- Before starting off, stand up in the coach and introduce the driver and yourself, then point out emergency exits.
- Sit down and start commentary.

En route

- Don't talk too much – keep looking back, and if clients are sleeping, they can't listen.
- At the beginning give brief outline of the day, approximate time of first meal or coffee-stop and local history – then into commentary.
- Repeat timings three times at stops. For example, 'We are stopping for coffee for 45 minutes. Please be back in the coach at 11.45; that is a quarter to twelve.' Give details of how to return to the coach if anyone gets lost or wants to go on their own. If pick-up is at a different location, make sure clients write down the place.
- At meals it may be best to sit with the driver. Again if you sit with a group you can cause jealousy, and you need a rest from questions otherwise you can't do your job properly. The only time this varies is with conference tours; you are acting as 'host' on the day and therefore you are on parade, even during lunch. The driver can escape and have lunch in the kitchen, but you have to be there to 'interpret' local table customs for guests who might be worried about etiquette, and want to watch you to see which fork you pick up first.
- Never forget the loo stop or souvenir shop. Visitors and these places are like dogs and lamp-posts – neither can go past without trying them out.
- Sit down once the coach is moving. We've all seen the guide standing up and guiding backwards – more fool them as visitors don't come to look at the guide, they

come to look at the scenery and buildings. Also if there is an accident the guide probably *won't* be covered for insurance purposes; they will be deemed to be contributorily negligent and could end up paralysed, and no insurance payable.

- Listen to yourself on the mike when you first test it – is it too loud or too soft – remember those at the back must be able to hear clearly. Vary the pitch and tone of your voice – use the nerves in the back of your neck or sit sideways so you can see the front clients' faces to get their reaction. *Never* give the same tour twice; always try out a new piece of information to see how it goes down, for your sanity and the client's interest.

- Point out and identify features. A good way is to liken the coach to a clock. 'On the left – at 9 o'clock – you can see . . .' Remember that people at the back of the coach have a restricted view.

- Stop talking when going past a beautiful view – or just to give clients a rest from your voice. As a rule of thumb a three-hour city tour means you probably have to speak for 50 minutes in an hour; on tour cut this down to 20 minutes every hour.

- At stops tell pax about photography and if there is a loo stop.

- Remind pax about local hazards – steps, uneven roads, pavements, cobble-stones, gangways, low ceilings, etc. before they leave the coach. Both for their own confidence and for insurance purposes.

- Talk to your pax and find out their interests – you might be able to point out something special to them, which they will remember all their life.

  Ask questions before about the group, so you can tailor your talk to *their* interests – not yours.

  Answer questions truthfully. If you don't know, say so – and find out.

- Coach loos are only to be used in an emergency. They can be the quickest way to spread food poisoning, etc., and with regular stops passengers don't need to use them.

- Use your sense of humour and smile – but don't make feeble or off-colour jokes.
- Use simple English and explain technical vocabulary.
- Keep to time. The group won't remember your deathless prose if they miss the ferry or are late for the theatre.
- Think about commentary content – strike a balance between educating and entertaining. Most visitors are interested in how people lived, rather than dates.
- Tell clients not to eat oranges while in the coach.
- Children can be some of the most rewarding passengers if you think about their needs.

Off the coach

- Explain 'local' rules, regarding e.g. dress; not to enter roped-off areas; not to touch objects – and why.
- Say where and when clients can take photos.
- Plan your tour to the slowest person in the group.
- Count your group at frequent intervals.
- With a large group, appoint a marker, e.g. a tall adult, to bring up the rear when walking clients around in a group.
- 'Throw' your voice to the person furthest at the back.
- Don't let your group stand if they can sit.
- Keep the group together – leave room for others to pass behind.
- Don't fidget – but do use positive hand gestures to point things out.
- Use eye contact.
- Choose stopping points carefully – do not obstruct other pedestrians or traffic, or talk near noisy places.
- Watch the group so they don't do anything stupid or dangerous.

On tour. When arriving at your evening hotel ask clients to stay on the coach while you go in to check. Hotels can move a group at the last minute. Valerie remembers climbing up hills to a German hotel way out in the country. Arriving, she went in to be met by an ashen-faced manager. 'You can't stay here tonight – the chef has just murdered the receptionist with his carving knife.'

Insurance.   Make sure you are adequately insured – don't rely on your employer – how do you know they have paid the premium?

Dress smartly.   The group may be students, but they've paid for a tour. Neatness, polished shoes, well-pressed clothes and attention to cleanliness gives an air of efficiency that inspire visitors' confidence in you. You are seen as the company representative, and therefore venues won't be impressed if you arrive on their doorstep scruffily dressed. They might forgive this from the clients – after all they are paying – but you are expected to know and follow local rules regarding dress.

Count, count and count again.   Every time passengers get back on the coach ensure that all of them are present.

Keep to your timetable.   The coach company won't be pleased if you are late and they miss another job or the driver goes over his/her hours.

Sloppy time-keeping = Bad guiding

Know the coach parks.   Be aware of any difficulties the driver may have.

House, site, museum and trail guides.   Ensure that you liaise with a tour leader to ensure they bring the group back on time, point out any areas of particular interest to the group, and collect a voucher if one is to be used instead of entrance fees. You may be giving a fascinating tour, with your group hanging on every word, but you won't get any thanks from the leader if you bring them back too late for their next appointment. Today's group tourists don't have the luxury of spending enough time at a site – so make sure they enjoy every minute of their visit and keep the leader happy. There are some guides who repeat the mantra 'It's such a pity your tour leader hasn't allowed enough time to see this city/site/building properly.' If you have to say this, you are a really bad guide. A five-minute overview of the site can be enough to set the scene indelibly in people's minds if the guide is good enough.

Mid-season blues

These happen to everyone, and the only cure is to go away for the day or a week and *totally* switch off. This is an interesting but stressful job, and you will find that once every season comes a group that you just can't get on with, and you aren't their idea of a guide. The best cure is to ask someone else to take over your tours for a short time, and go far away from crowds. When your bounce is back then return to wow them!

Summary

Your group will remember their visit with pleasure if you are

* able to make places come alive,
* informative,
* interesting, and
* entertaining.

5 Training

Is training really necessary?

One day Valerie was working at an exhibition, and was approached by a tour operator who asked her if she would like to take a group of his clients to Italy.

'I've never been to Italy,' said Valerie.

'Well, now's the time to go,' said Sam.

'But I don't know anything about the country.'

'Now's the time to learn.' And off went Valerie as tour manager in charge of a group of unsuspecting tourists. On her first trip, she didn't even know how to use a mike, and turned beetroot red with embarrassment every time she had to make an announcement.

Once, like Valerie, you were often thrown onto a coach with no training. Today, companies have to hire staff with the right training and experience, otherwise they risk being sued under the EU Directive (more about this later on). It can be a Catch-22 situation, with companies demanding trained staff, but few training courses. Working in Europe you will need a certificate to satisfy the national police that you have a qualification entitling you to work in their country (more about this later).

Working at a stately home, as a site guide, trail guide, etc., you will be given a training course. Some are very cursory, some excellent.

If you want to work as a guide with local walking or coach tours then you will need to take an officially approved training course.

Once, as a trained guide, if you moved and wanted to work in another area you had to take another course. In future, if you possess an S/NVQ or approved qualification, you will just add on appropriate local knowledge.

Where do you find training?

For tour managers
- The Netherlands has a two-year management course in tourism and recreation at Breda.
- In Britain some colleges offer basic training.
- In London and a few centres in Britain you can take a short course for an OCR qualification.
- Distance-learning courses.

For guides
- Through regional tourist boards or local authorities.
- There are some courses for NVQs at Levels 2 and 3 being offered in colleges. Ask your local regional tourist board which they recognize.
- For specialized guiding, courses at adult education centres, museums and galleries, OCR courses, etc. are available. Join these up with a basic course.

First aid
This is necessary for many courses and jobs. Most will check that you have taken a course covering emergency aid with CPR, or cardio-pulmonary resuscitation, i.e. what to do if someone has a heart attack, etc. rather than first aid dealing with broken limbs.

At the top of a mountain or in the wilds of a forest, if someone has a suspected heart attack there are simple steps you can take that might save their lives, long before medical assistance can reach them. If they break a leg, on the other hand, provided you keep them warm and reassure them, they can usually wait for professional assistance to help strap up their limbs before moving them.

What should a basic course cover?

Tour managers

The IATM have developed Core Competency standards for tour managers, which include:

Understanding the tourism industry, including the socio-economic importance of tourism and responsible tourism; Assessing needs and expectations of clients; Preparing for tour; Confirming reservations; Developing and tailoring commentaries to tour and client; Using communication systems effectively and clearly; Non-verbal communication; Identifying the importance of adhering to an itinerary; First-day tour briefing; Welcome and farewell gathering; Checking in at transportation terminals and hotels; Seat rotation; Supervising clients; Handling international border crossings; Providing navigation to coach driver; Selling optionals; Supervising baggage; Tour reports, cash control and reporting procedures; Problem handling; Responding to emergencies; Safety and security; Handling upgrades, comps and commissions; Managing stress; Maintaining positive working relationships with driver, local tourist guides, etc.; Following guidelines for cross-cultural awareness; Responding to clients with special needs; Legislation; Identifying types of information required; Map reading; Handling bumping; etc.

Guides

Guides will need to learn local history, geography and about the local economy; how to do transfers if appropriate; how to research; delivering appropriate commentaries for day tours, walking tours, museum, site and coach tour guiding; historical knowledge; local geography; economics; basic emergency aid; EC law; health and safety; customer care; handling special groups; environmental issues; body language; personal awareness; how to read a map, etc.

Training is never wasted, but some courses are not answering trainees' needs and you must make sure you choose the right course for the work you want to do. A recent government-funded report from the Business Tourism Forum said, 'degree courses, offered by college and universities, produce management graduates but not the range of skills and levels needed for the "nuts and bolts" of the industry', and went on to highlight the need to focus on a 'bottom-up' approach for the first steps to training.

First steps

The English Tourism Council's series of 'Welcome' courses are a useful introduction.

Take a first aid course.

Take a distance-learning course. Leisure World Training Company's course tapes cover the theory of transfers, check-ins, hospitality desks, selling excursions and working in the industry. Tapes were developed by operators, tour managers, guides, representatives and meet-and-greet staff, so when the tapes talk about problem-solving, they have 'been there, seen it, done it'.

Investigate taking an S/NVQ.

What are NVQs?

National Vocational Qualifications (SVQs in Scotland) are nationally recognized qualifications showing you have the practical skills to work in the sector. Based on national standards set by industry for industry, they are recognized by employers as proof of your ability.

To obtain a qualification you build up units of competence, i.e. you prove you can do a certain vocational task needed in your job, and are judged competent to carry out this task.

These units can be 'mixed and matched' to build up NVQs. You may already have carried out work to the standard required in another job; this can be used for APL (accreditation of prior learning) – which you use to obtain a unit towards an NVQ.

You don't work through a course and take an exam at the end. Instead you are taught on the modular system, until you have completed enough units for an NVQ.

Warning. We may be part of Europe, but the QCA (Qualifications and Curriculum Authority that administer NVQs) don't seem to realize that Britain is part of the EU. NVQ qualifications don't yet answer the EU CEN/TC 329/WG2's requirements for working in Europe! So if you are going to work as a tour manager in Europe, current qualifications are offered by the Institute of Tourism and Transport Studies (NHTV) in Holland, and the OCR qualification (which was designed on NVQ lines to slot into the framework).

Why is it necessary to have a qualification to work in Europe?
In simplistic terms, it is all about 'protectionism'. Known as 'I don't want you working in my patch taking work away from me.'

For years guides were rewarded by a regular supply of tour groups wanting a guide to take them around. Today, that picture is changing. The regular 'milk run' tours (visiting the best-known places) are in decline. Tourists are becoming more adventurous. Their friends have been on tour, and returned to say 'don't do that – you only meet other tourists'.

Today, groups no longer stay for several days in one city. Tourists are bored of going round Rome or Paris, following a crocodile of visitors. Instead, operators are offering more interesting and adventurous tours – many visiting villages and unknown areas. This means less work for the local official guides, and more for tour managers with a flexible attitude over the knowledge they must acquire before each tour to satisfy the expectations of these 'new' clients.

So the local guide sees coaches roaring through their area, but no longer stopping so they can step on and give visitors a guided commentary. They feel they are resident in the area and obviously know it better than a visitor, so they should be the person to talk about it. However, visitors are quite content to have someone give them an overview of an area focusing on their particular interests. Generally they prefer to have the same person all the time; they become used to their delivery, and that person understands their demands.

So it is not surprising that when Brussels produced a Directive on mutuality of qualifications that guides latched on to that, and started to ask the local police to check that anyone in charge of a visiting coach had the right qualifications.

Industry media have been full of stories of tour managers being stopped and questioned, then having to go to the local police station and prove their company considers them competent to look after their clients. Eventually tour managers receive this assurance, but it takes time; and clients are left waiting. Today tour mangers can prove their competence by producing an IATM or OCR Certificate.

Training for tour managers

Currently the most comprehensive course is the two-year course run by the Netherlands Institute of Tourism and Transport Studies (NHTV) in Breda, Holland, which includes units designed in co-operation with the Dutch department of the IATM.

The core part of the course covers a general knowledge of travel agency and tour operations, marketing and management, then goes into geography and ethnology, history and history of art, day-to-day routine and all the practical aspects of conducting a tour, communication skills such as how to handle groups, salesmanship, how to deal with complaints, how to negotiate and give a presentation, psychology, political economy, etc.

In addition, students have the opportunity to obtain a first aid certificate.

The native language of the students is Dutch. Beside English, the students choose two of the following languages: French, Italian, Spanish or German.

The only way to acquire skills is by practising them, and this is therefore the main objective of many of the lessons. After theoretical knowledge has been acquired by the students through self-study, they get ample opportunity to practise the various skills during the lessons.

During their second year at Breda students have to plan, organize and conduct a five-day tour to a European destination. This tour has to meet a number of requirements such as sights to be seen and working visits to be paid. And during the second year, the last term has been reserved for an internship.

The course has no final examinations: all the results gained by the students during the two years will decide whether they receive the diploma.

In Britain, the Tourism Training Organisation (TTO) and

some colleges run courses that lead to an OCR Certificate (Oxford, Cambridge and RSA). For a certificate, trainees need to study transfers, tour management, walking, site and coach tours, specialized guiding, eco-tourism, working at conferences and exhibitions, social history, body language, researching commentaries, using a mike, basic Emergency Aid, EC law, health and safety, customer care, personal awareness, etc. and include visits to an international airport, and walking and coach tours.

If you don't live near a suitable college it is possible to take some of the course as a distance-learning module, offered by Leisure World Training Company, and then come to London for an intensive course offered by TTO.

NVQs for guides

Regional tourist boards in England have been involved in developing NVQs which will eventually take the place of the regional tourist board guide qualification, known as Blue or Green Badges from the colour of the badge.

Since the Festival of Britain the tourist boards and various other bodies have been supporting guide training and its advancement. In the mid-1980s the government introduced the concept of NVQs, and from 1999 courses supporting the achievement of NVQs (at Level 4) are gradually being introduced by the regional tourist boards. Due to supply and demand variations, some regions will run courses more frequently than others.

To start on the vocational qualification route, apply to your local tourist board (telephone the ETC if you don't know their address). Currently courses are set up as follows (although this may change as NVQs evolve).

Priority for places on a programme will normally be given to those who speak appropriate languages fluently. Next comes an interview to set out the work and study that is involved, as well as ensuring that your hopes and aspirations from guiding are both realistic and pitched at the appropriate level of necessary qualification.

Programmes start with an induction day explaining concepts of NVQs. Then candidates are required to achieve Welcome

Host and Welcome All qualifications, intended to ingrain high standards of customer service as a foundation. Both programmes have been widely recognized for their quality and value, with Welcome All tackling vital issues associated with service for those with disabilities or specific needs. It is necessary to understand these matters, not least in appreciating legal requirements under the terms of the Disability Discrimination Act. Welcome Host is the most popular programme for achieving qualification in customer service of any in the country.

Next is a communications skills module, assessing ability in presentation and taking account of the special circumstances of the guiding experience. There is a chance to improve learning skills and techniques with the creation of evidence that contributes to NVQ success.

After, tutors may talk with candidates to advise them if it is apparent that they will make the grade as a guide, or not. This is intended to be helpful and save trainees wasting time and money on a course, if it is not suitable for them.

Next is a distance-learning course, supported by tutorials and seminars. You are presented with five very smart files covering:

- Geography and tourism
- Monarchy, government and law
- History and religion
- Health, local government and education
- Arts, culture, media and sport

You then carry out your own research on these subjects. This will involve visiting venues, and research in your local library.

What about the Internet? It is useful for background, but do check, check and treble-check its information. Your clients will want accurate details, and currently much that is put on the Internet has not been checked.

So if you are the person who does their research sitting in front of a screen – go no further. Your first group of intelligent tourists will suss you out. In this job you make a friend of your local librarian, and gradually build up your own research library.

Sophie says, 'I use the library constantly. If I find a book that gives me good information, I then go out and buy it. I counted up last night and find I have over 800 books I use for work.' Books she and others recommend are listed at the end of this book.

Part of the course is a business skills module. Most guiding jobs are for self-employed people and it is vital to know how to sell and market your guiding service. There are several assignments to complete, including the development of a personal business/marketing plan. Incidentally, if you come from a business background you may be credited with APL (Accreditation of Prior Learning).

Next, it's on to regional knowledge covering tourism trends, history, geography and associated topics, supplemented by seminars and tutorials.

You must be enthusiastic to complete the course; if you get a thrill standing where Prince Rupert led one of his famous cavalry charges during the Civil War, or underneath the room where Fleming discovered penicillin, and can enthuse your visitors, this job could be for you.

The final part of the programme is a series of practical tuition days, covering walking tours, coach guiding and looking after visitors in museums and 'sensitive' venues such as churches. Then a final assessment, demonstrating that you can bring together all of the components of good guiding in a real situation. Assessors will look to see that all of the practical learning and depth of understanding is being applied and, if successful, the planned procedure in each region is the award of the Regional Blue Badge. This entitles the holder to become a Registered Guide with their tourist board.

However, you are still learning. To achieve the Level 4 NVQ you will start working, and need to produce evidence obtained 'on the job', including feedback from tourists and operators who have been customers of your service.

This entire process is expected to take two years.

If you find your regional tourist board doesn't offer a current programme of study – or if this is over-subscribed – an alternative may be a college programme either at Level 2 and 3, or the OCR Diploma.

How is it done in Scotland?
The Scottish guides' course takes two academic years of part-time study and consists of:

- Core knowledge including geology, archaeology, history, architecture, literature/music, environment.
- Professional guiding skills: a total of 17 practical days including 6 formative assessment days. Personal research and familiarization is expected for all courses.
- Detailed area studies: 6 areas – 17 days including 6 days for practical training.

On successful completion of the training programme, there is a four-day examination to ensure overall competence as a self-employed tourist guide capable of a wide variety of customer-tailored tours, qualified to guide throughout Scotland.

In some Highland and Island areas there have been short introductory training courses to meet local needs. Local area guides have a minimum of six days training, in addition to personal study and written work and have a one-day practical assessment.

The STGA continues discussions with Scottish universities and natural environment agencies for future course development.

The STGA say that to act as an ambassador for Scotland a guide needs: enthusiasm, motivation, warmth, stamina, confidence, innovation, flexibility, clarity of speech, ability to communicate and fluency in a foreign language.

Wales
On the application form to become a guide in the Principality, you have to state why you wish to train as a guide, and describe the qualities and characteristics which you think will make *you* a good guide.

The tourist board's course offers a training in

- guiding techniques, presentation and communication skills on site, on foot and on coach
- general UK national knowledge
- Welsh knowledge

and covers history, geology, geography and environment, industry and commerce, finance and taxation, literature, law, architecture, religion, monarchy and government, visual and performing arts, education and health, sport, tourism, and business and marketing skills.

Currently, the course takes place for one week in November, two to three days in February and another week in March. Each section takes place in a different area of Wales, and in between there is structured home study, project work and research for the practicals which are an essential part of the course.

It is often difficult to find employers to give up time to help with training, which can mean steering groups and exam panels consisting of guides rather than operators. Perhaps operators should think about giving up some time to ensure that guides are trained for today's visitor expectations.

Regional guide training

While the regions are changing over to vocational training, there may be some courses offering traditional training.

In the east of England region there are ten locations with enough work for part-time guides: Bury St Edmunds, Cambridge, Colchester, Ely, Ipswich, King's Lynn, Norwich, Peterborough, Uttlesford and St Albans.

Anyone selected to attend a training course sponsored by the Board must be prepared to spend some ten hours a week in private study over the period of the course. The training course consists of local knowledge (which may be open to local residents in addition to potential guides), national knowledge (core subjects as laid down by the English Tourism Council), and presentation training to deliver tours on foot, on site and on a coach.

After successfully completing a year as a town/city guide you can apply to attend a course covering the whole of the east of England.

Warnings

Guide courses are a popular option for colleges faced with needing to improve their sales, or availability of learning programmes. Before you sign up for *any* tourism course, ask:

- Is it endorsed or recognized by a tourist board, the Travel Training Company (ABTA's training arm) or an association?
- Does it issue a qualification recognized by a tourist board or one of the recognized assessment authorities (City and Guilds, OCR)?
- Is teaching delivered by those with genuine industry experience?
- What is the teachers' level of contact with the industry?
- Have the teachers worked in the industry?

Ask – and if the answer is vague, go elsewhere. It's your money – don't be a dropout from a bad course.

Beware the college course offering IATA or BA fares and ticketing as training for guides. Normally, tour managers and guides don't sell airline seats!

There should be help on how to market yourself and find work. Ask if the course gives any help with finding jobs. If teachers have worked in the industry, they will know where the jobs are to be found. It's no guarantee of employment – but it's a start.

Warning! Speaking to the Travel Training Company, they say they are often asked about overpriced college courses; sadly this usually happens after trainees have paid for the course. These courses offer fares and ticketing, IT and computer studies, and a course diploma for 'tour guide work', but very little or no training on a coach. Fares and ticketing are necessary for travel agency staff, but not for tour managers or guides. Although many tour managers carry a laptop with them, and guides use computers to do their accounts and send letters, there are more important elements that should be taught on a course. So if you have any doubts about a course – *ask*.

One college advertises a diploma in tour guide operations. They say this consists of 'tour guide work', ticketing and

computer studies – and costs nearly £4,000. Why include ticketing and computer studies, rather than suitable lectures for guiding? 'Because we teach them.' When phoned they didn't know
the name of the tutor in charge, but offered 'a college diploma at
the end of the course' – not a recognized qualification.

For the moment NVQs are only accepted informally in some
European countries; so if you are working as a tour manager in
Europe, carry an IATM or OCR certificate. Plans are afoot to
found an Institute for guides, which should do much to improve
acceptance of qualifications.

Under 18?

If you are keen to become a guide, but find that course
organizers insist that you must be older, you can take a basic
GNVQ (General National Vocational Qualification) or distance-
learning course. Read the *Intermediate Textbook for GNVQ
Leisure and Tourism*, published by Addison Wesley Longman
(ISBN 0-582-27841-4) as a good basic guide to the tourism
industry. It explains tachographs, the EU Directive, health and
safety issues, and how the industry works.

Previously, GNVQs received the thumbs-down from employers, so the QCA (Quality and Curriculum Authority) have
recently had the units rewritten. OCR (Oxford, Cambridge and
RSA) and City & Guilds examining boards have employed
people working in the industry to write the new units, and you
might find their optional unit on conferences and events is
particularly helpful.

Finding that charity work is often a useful factor on a CV,
this GNVQ unit asks students to plan a charity event such as a
flag day for a recognized charity like the RNLI, Guide Dogs for
the Blind, SARDA, etc. The idea is that if you have actually
helped plan a flag day, negotiating for selling space and finding
flag-sellers, and have liaised with the police, and then made a
profit for the charity – you obviously have the basics of what it
takes to work for a tourism company.

A distance-learning course can also give you a good insight
into the industry, and as Maria Bertorelli of Thomsons said, 'it
proves you have invested in yourself'.

Then go off and try for work with a local stately home or

venue where they offer 'interpretation' jobs and often welcome younger staff, particularly if school groups make a large part of their visitors.

Specialized courses

What happens if you want to work with specialized groups? Groups interested in art, history of art, architecture, who share a hobby, play a sport – or any of a thousand different interests?

Once they have taken a basic course, and perhaps have worked for a season or two, some people will go on to take courses so they can offer tours on a specialized subject.

Others come into guiding already having a specialist skill or knowledge. For example, architects interested in guiding are often in demand, particularly from conference organizers who plan post-conference tours aimed at their delegates' interests. If you want to see how this is done, and you are in London, a firm called Architectural Dialogue runs tours at weekends. They show different perspectives of the city, highlighting 'unknown' buildings.

Cricket fans might have noticed the new media stand at Lords, looking like something out of a science fiction film. You can see this, and the hallowed turf of Lords, on one of their tours. (0208 341 1371)

Case study

Arthur retired having worked for an engineering company, ending up as marketing director. Once retired, he found he was bored. There were limits to the amount of time he could work in the garden, or watch cricket. A friend suggested, why not look after the many visitors who came to the local city? 'You enjoy history, and told us fascinating stories about cricket in its early days,' said one of his friends. Another friend said, 'Phone Molly, she took a basic guiding course in London.'

Molly was enthusiastic. 'It gave me confidence. We had come from all over the country, and the course gave us a solid grounding in the basics – we had to find out our own information to tell visitors – but I enjoyed it, and the tutor was very helpful in telling me where to find work.'

Arthur took the same course, enjoying being back in the classroom. Their tutor showed the class the basics and how to build on their expertise to look after visitors: 'After all, you have all done something interesting with your lives, and visitors can relate to your experiences.'

To develop interesting commentaries, 'use your library,' they were told, and when given a walking tour of the area around their classroom, Arthur was astonished to know how much you can find out if you really know where to look. Their on-course assessment consisted of organizing a tour to an area they had never visited. 'This will often happen to you in your career. Once you have actually done it you will know you can.' They were all dreading the day, but using their research, what they had been taught and commonsense, they ended up having a wonderful tour, 'and it gave me a real sense of achievement' Arthur told his wife that evening.

Using the course list of tour-operating SMEs (small and medium enterprises), Arthur started phoning. He reckons he made over one hundred phone calls before a conference organizer asked him if he would take a walking tour of his city for a group that were attending a meeting. She wanted the tour 'before dinner – about 6 to 7.30 p.m., and they would like to see the museum with its collection of embroideries.' Arthur was just about to say the museum closed at 5 p.m., when he saw his wife frantically waving at him. He said he would call the organizer back, and asked his wife why she had been signalling. 'I was speaking to Joan the other day, and she says the museum is keen to host groups after hours – for a supplement.'

Now Arthur is building up his walking tours, and has found that his newly gained knowledge of embroidery brings him in two or three specialized tours a month. He enjoys his 'retirement' so much that he is thinking of taking an NVQ, especially as he will probably gain APL for what he has already learnt.

Sophie's path

Having completed a course to become a registered (Blue Badge) guide, Sophie has the basic knowledge, but wants to know more. She finds out that her favourite museum, the Victoria and Albert (V&A) run courses based on their world-famous collections, lasting from one day to a year. Colleagues told her the courses are excellent, giving an in-depth background and lots of useful information. One-day study days cover costume design and fashion, Chinese ceramics, sculpture, etc. One-month short courses cover history of art and architecture; and generally two one-year courses take place every year – offering Renaissance or modern art.

The V&A also offers fascinating drop-in workshops, and even if you don't take a course it is useful to belong to the Friends. Their year-long certificate course costs £1,259, but much as Sophie would love to do this, she has too much work booked. However, she now takes regular one-day and short courses, which stimulate her brain and give her 'lots and lots of information to help make my tours more interesting'. (More details, 0207 938 8638.)

Conferences and events

Many tour managers and guides work on conference tours, but companies stress that they need staff who can relate to their clients, not bore them rigid with too much information. 'They've been there, seen it, done it and don't need "tourist" information,' says Diana. If tour managers like meticulous administration and creativity, it is often possible to find a full-time job in this sector. For new staff, 'most of us find the best way is in-house training we give our staff so that they learn to do things our way'.

The Association of British Professional Conference Organisers run courses each year. 'These again were initiated for their own staff but are generally available and those wishing to be included on the list should contact them on (01480) 496603'.

Conservation and wildlife

English Nature run excellent walks on their reserves, led by site managers and staff who have an in-depth knowledge, providing useful information to include in tour commentaries. There is probably a reserve near you, offering some fascinating days out, ranging from two-hour strolls to day-long walks.

Subjects covered include charcoal burning in Cornwall; using a map and compass in County Durham (very useful); 'Bogs are beautiful' in Cumbria; guided walks in Derbyshire, Hampshire and Devon; tree trails in Gloucestershire; fen wildlife in Norfolk; bugs in Oxford; hay meadow flowers in Staffordshire and wildlife and management in Worcestershire.

If you like the countryside, or even if you loathe it, when working as a tour manager the walks can add to your basic knowledge, and help you to explain to visitors the work that is being done to conserve our Earth heritage. One of English Nature's aims is to raise public awareness and understanding of our countryside and its wildlife, and the reserves are always keen to host visiting groups. Their enquiry service publishes excellent and helpful leaflets – (01733) 455100.

Ski guides

In Europe, especially in France, you must take an approved course if you want to be a ski guide, taking visitors out on the different runs on- and off-piste. Otherwise, as newspaper reports will testify, you can be slung in jail. Even with training, accidents can happen. Led by one of the best ski guides in the world, Prince Charles and his party were still caught in a fatal avalanche.

At the French Savoy resort of La Rosière, Henri Joly explained that he had nothing against hiring British staff to work as instructors and guides, provided that they had taken an approved course which taught not only the techniques but also how to read the weather. In fact he said he welcomed English-speaking staff, as he introduced me to Sam. Working the season at La Rosière, Sam had gone through the 'tough but fair' French training. 'You have to be able to speak French fluently, and once the locals realize you are serious, they are tremendously supportive and helpful.'

Guided walks on snowshoes are becoming increasingly popular in the Alps, and at La Rosière, Richard takes visitors around in the winter, doing everything from showing off bird tracks in the snow, to giving visitors an insight into life in an Alpine village. He takes the same tours in the summer, but wearing ordinary boots!

How to find a course

Mark wanted to work in tourism showing people around. 'Told I needed a training course, I found lots that offered training to be a travel agent. Speaking to the teachers I told them that I wanted to deal with people, showing them around. My local college said what I wanted was their course which included fares and ticketing. This sounded a good idea, until I happened to talk to a coach driver. I told him I wanted to work on coaches and was going to do a travel agent's course. He soon put me right, telling me this was useless for what I wanted to do.

'But won't fares and ticketing be useful?'

'If I have ever seen a tour manager or guide issue a plane ticket, you can call me an idiot' was his comment. 'Wait a minute, I am meeting a group off this train and they will have someone in charge – ask them.' And I did. That is how I came to take a course for an OCR Certificate.

On the course, our tutor, Michelle, gave us a list of hundreds of companies, and I started phoning – and phoning – and phoning. I swear I made a thousand phone calls, but actually it was probably about a hundred. Eventually I found a local coach company who wanted someone to take a tour to the Christmas Market in Cologne in Germany.

On our course we had been issued with a tape on hotel check-ins, and I played this the night before we left so I could remember what I had to do. Then I checked everyone, and their luggage, carefully before we set off. However, the tour wasn't what I imagined at all. For a start, my carefully prepared notes on German history lay in my pocket. All my clients wanted me to do was explain what happened about buying 'duty free' on the ferry.

Luckily I had been across to France a month before with my father to buy wine for a family anniversary party, so I knew what passengers could purchase now that technically 'duty free' is abolished. However, 'duty paid' goods on the ferries are almost as good value, and the driver and I promised we would stop at a French hypermarket on the return journey.

My first group were a good lot. Not at all demanding and determined to have a good time, but was I thankful that I had paid attention on my training course! I began to see what the EU Directive was all about, as I made sure my clients got what they had paid for, and checked and double-checked everything.

It rained all the first day, but luckily Michelle had thought of this, and given us all ideas on being creative. 'Don't use tapes,' we were told. That is lazy guiding. I gave a talk about the way Belgians liked their beer and how many different varieties there were, then set the group a sophisticated version of 'I spy', one side of the coach playing against the other side spotting adverts and pub signs: one point for a Belgian beer, two for a German one, three for a British or other foreign beer.

Next day everyone spent their time shopping. In the evening we had a trip to a wine cellar along with six other coaches from the same company. The cellar looked like a big warehouse, but luckily the clients couldn't see much as we arrived, and inside it was decorated with plastic hops and barrels. Wine was unlimited, so everyone had a good time and all were on the coach when it was time to leave. Some of the other coaches were very delayed as their tour managers tried to round up their group. Luckily Michelle had warned us this might happen, and before we arrived I told my group that it didn't matter if anyone wanted to stay on after the end of the evening. The driver had to leave bang on the dot because of his driving hours, and we would take everyone back who was on the coach. For those who wanted to stay, a taxi back to the hotel would only cost about £50. They were all waiting on the coach!

After this tour I was asked to do more work: a trip to Disneyland taking a group by Eurostar; several evening trips to the theatre and dinner; and Paris and Amsterdam weekends. Gradually the tours I was offered became more up-market, where clients wanted me to give them commentaries on history. I decided to sign up for a history course at the local adult education centre.

Once I had a winter season under my belt, I started phoning some of the companies on my jobs list that said they only employed experienced tour managers, and now I have regular work taking groups around Europe. I hope to take some groups to the States next summer – and then who knows; perhaps China or Australia?

To find out more about training, contact your regional tourist board, your local tourist information centre, the Travel Training Company or Tourism Training Company.

Become a volunteer
Many museums welcome volunteers to take visitors around, and this is one way of learning 'on the job' if you can't take time off, or afford a course. In the London Transport Museum guided tours are carried out by volunteers at weekends and on bank holidays. These volunteers have to be members of the Friends of London Transport Museum, and currently membership costs £15 per year (0207 379 6344).

Loans
To pay for a course, you can take out a career development loan. These loans help applicants pay for vocational training by offering a deferred-repayment bank loan. You can borrow between £300 and £8,000 to pay for up to 80 per cent of course fees, plus the full cost of books, materials and other related expenses.

The course has to be related to the work you want to do, and generally not last more than two years (0800 585 505).

Contacts for some other courses

Jersey Tourism (01534) 500743.
Leisure World Training Co. (distance-learning) (01295) 273574.
London Tourist Board 0207 932 2039.
OCR Course 0207 351 4434.
Orkney Guiding Services (01856) 811777.
Yorkshire Tourist Board (01904) 707961.

If you don't know your regional tourist board's telephone number, either ask you local TIC (tourist information centre) or look under Helpful Contacts at the back of this book.

Northumbria Tourist Board and Hadrian's Wall Partnership offered a pilot scheme for NVQs at Levels 2 and 3 to candidates during the spring and summer of 1999. For future details phone Val Wooff at 0191–375 3018.

Qualifications

As mentioned before, the new NVQs are not currently compatible with European requirements, as they don't meet CEN/TC 329/WG2's critera (see Chapter 11).

The Netherlands College of Travel and Tourism examination (held under the auspices of IATM) is in two parts: a written examination (multiple-choice style) and an oral examination before a panel made up of the teaching staff of Breda College, management of a coach operator, tour operators, board of IATM and possibly a hotel regularly used by tour groups.

To take this certificate you must be a graduate of Breda College with at least 60 days' experience as a tour manager, or have enough experience to qualify as a full member of IATM.

The OCR (Oxford, Cambridge and RSA) qualification is a certificate (equivalent to Level 2). If you have worked in the industry you will gain a diploma (Level 3). Before you use this in Europe or elsewhere in the world you must have it verified by the appropriate authorities that accept the qualification (Italian, German, Brazilian, etc.).

To work at certain sites in Britain (e.g. Edinburgh Castle,

Windsor Castle, Tower of London), you will need a regional or NVQ qualification, a 'Blue Badge' or regional 'Green Badge'.

Other countries have their own qualifications for registered guides; ask their local embassy for details.

What does a course cost?

Like the length of a piece of string, this is difficult to answer. However, the Scottish Guides give the following guidelines. These are only estimates, and may change with inflation, demands of S/NVQs, etc.

Interview and language assessment	£30
Introductory course	£160
Core knowledge £35 to £99 per unit	£350–£600
Area studies	£1,200
Professional guiding skills 2 × £228	£556
Final examination	£300

Allowance must be made on any course for books – the basis of your personal library, plus additional travel and meals on personal research trips.

Courses for an OCR qualification are shorter, and cost around £600. But of course these don't go into nearly so much detail.

6 Running a training course

'It's the training that's at fault – why don't you put in a chapter about how to run a good training course, then we might have staff that relate better to our groups?'

Sam and Charlie were sitting in the Meridien Club at World Travel Market, grumbling about finding the right guides. They felt a big fault was that 'many courses are organized by guides as trainers, with no input from tourists or tour operators'.

'And another thing,' the two operators started to voice their grievances: 'a guide course is *not* a tour manager course'. The jobs differ, and colleges should emphasize the difference, although they should cover both. The Scottish guide training found favour with them both, 'probably because their guides have to do touring as well – which is reflected in the training'. Otherwise 'there is very little training for tour managers – currently only Breda and the OCR course,' said Charlie. 'But what about colleges offering training?' Charlie snorted. 'Most are run by teachers who have done a student job as a rep., and think they know it all,' was his verdict.

'Anyone running a training course should first ask the average tourist in the street what they want,' according to Charlie. 'That driver in the TV *Tourist Trouble* programme put his finger on one of the biggest problems of guiding: timing. It is vitally important that this is drummed into trainees on a course,' although he and Sam agreed that this wasn't so much of a problem in Europe. Guides there seem to have a more pragmatic approach: if they have been told to carry out an hour's tour, why should they work longer if the client doesn't want this?

Then out came their wish-list of what teachers should teach:

Timing

'I often have to organize a sightseeing tour in-between a meeting and dinner – but can the guide keep to an hour? No.'

Repeating that with any tour, timing is of the utmost importance, Sam and Charlie were of the opinion that training guides to guide backwards was part of the fault – 'they don't have their eyes on what is happening'.

True. Going up St James's in London the guide was telling us about London's clubland, while in front was the Harrods coach drawn by two horses. Of course passengers were pointing this out – while the guide droned on oblivious of what was happening behind his back! And if you aren't reminded of the time by passing clocks, it might explain bad time-keeping.

The Scottish course teaches guides to guide on the coach looking forwards, and to be aware of visual priorities.

Frances is a travel writer based in London who writes pieces for the *Washington Post* and other prestigious US papers.

Frequently on press trips us journalists are sitting in the coach reminding the guide that time is pressing, and we have an important appointment; but the guide takes no notice. In Tunisia we were so furious as our trip got more and more behind on timing, that one of us said we had left something in the last hotel and asked the guide to find it. As soon as the guide got off the coach we told the driver to drive straight to our next appointment. With a grin, he followed our instructions. For once we arrived in time, having missed out what the guide had said 'You *must* see,' and it didn't make any difference to our stories which we had travelled all those miles to write.

And I have lost count of the number of times we are told by our hosts that we will arrive back at our hotel at 5.30. This should give us time before we have to be on parade again to phone editors, dash off a correction, pick up messages and have a quick shower.

Now my heart sinks when I see on the programme: 'Your Blue Badge Guide will accompany you.' Often this means the guide never stops talking, we arrive back an hour late and miss the chance to freshen up before we go off again: no wonder journalists look so scruffy! And those bits added in are never included in our copy. With tight wordage restrictions, we are only able to write about the important sights in our destination reports.

Why can't they all be like Anne in Edinburgh? She gave us a wonderful tour on New Year's Eve, managed to include special snippets aimed at all our different types of readers, and brought us back to the hotel with ten minutes to spare. We loved her! Otherwise send the press officer to look after us; they know anecdotes that keep our copy fresh, and they have a vested interest in getting us back on time.

Standing up

This was another *bête noir* for the duo. They don't want staff to stand up while guiding. 'Visitors have come to see the country – not the guide. I don't mind the tour manager or guide who carefully works their way down the coach aisle, answering questions from clients, provided they hold on,' says Sam. 'My insurance company says staff aren't covered if they break the law – and standing up in a moving coach is against the law in most countries.'

One guide was very surprised to be sacked from Ambassadors of Britain, a guide-booking agency. She had been caught sitting on the ledge in front of the coach windscreen while she guided, and warned this was dangerous and that a repeat meant instant dismissal. Driving round Parliament Square her boss happened to be in a passing taxi. Next minute the guide was surprised to find her driver stopping. Her boss asked her to step outside, and told her in no uncertain terms that she was impeding the driver's view, to collect her belongings, and her boss would take over. The driver was sitting there with a big grin on his face: 'I kept on asking her to sit down, but she wouldn't.'

On the Continent drivers generally won't start driving until the guide is sitting down.

CCTV

Recently Charlie had been asked to be an examiner, and had some very interesting observations about closed-circuit TV being

used for training. 'It can be inhibiting. People being filmed
aren't looking objectively to find out what they can improve.
Reality is that they think they look fat, or don't like the clothes
they are wearing, or think their make-up is ghastly. They end
up being embarrassed and lose their spontaneity.' The Tourism
Training Organisation obtained the coveted ABTA seal of
approval, and they agree. 'We were given a grant to use CCTV,
but decided against using it a second time – we found it
counter-productive. Help and advice from teachers on the
course, and even better from their peers over coffee, works much
better. Instead of CCTV we budget for more sessions on the
coach.'

Coaches
Training must be on a 40-foot coach; there is a big difference in
mike feedback between a small 'puddle jumper' and a big coach.
Michelle runs a booking agency for a coach tour operator and
also trains tours managers and guides. 'One of my clients needs
50 guides a season for their different tours. They look to me to
book people who know how to handle groups. I always insist on
using a 36- or 40-foot coach on training days. A mini-coach
may save money for the course organizers, but it is useless for
training. The feedback on the mike is totally different, and
trainees need to be able to gauge space so they don't ask drivers
to park where the coach won't fit in.'

Anyone thinking of taking a training course should ask the
college if they use a full-sized coach on training days.

Marketing
Charlie and Sam have a scale of fees based on guidelines from
their local tourist board, but guides can earn bonuses which
increase earnings. 'But don't tell readers how much they can
earn; it will encourage those only in it for the money.' But
earnings are equivalent to those of a PA, and even better for
someone at the top of the tree.

Any course should include a strong element of how trainees
can market themselves, and provide lists of potential employers,
'and not the same companies who are on the hit-list of any new
guides. Be creative. Teachers working in the industry should

know what 'new' companies are looking for staff, and suggest how trainees can use their skills to work for different types of tour operators. *Working in Tourism* has a directory of over 300 companies (ISBN 1-85458-218-6, £11.95).

EU Directive

Everything operators do, from brochure planning to tour organization, is governed by this Directive. 'Even though many of your tours are to countries outside the EU?' I asked.

'Any tour sold in the EU, even if the destination is outside the European Union, is governed by the EU Directive on Package Travel. That is why it is so important that the basic principles are taught on any course.'

The Directive requires accuracy for brochure descriptions: therefore tour managers and guides must ensure that they follow the itinerary as stated in brochures; accommodation as promised, ditto ferries and other transport; no changes to what is written in the brochure unless this follows certain guidelines; the operator has a duty of care to clients, and their representatives (tour managers and guides) must ensure clients receive what they have paid for.

Alan Bowen was head of ABTA's legal department when the Directive was in negotiation. He believes that the Directive is 'good housekeeping', and everyone working in this industry must understand the basic principles. US legislation is also tough, following the same basic EU Directive's principles of customer care and looking after your clients.

It is so important that staff understand what is required by the Directive, otherwise clients can sue a company, and win thousands in compensation. 'If they have paid for a certain holiday, and elements change, they won't get that time back, so their long-awaited break could be ruined,' said Charlie.

Administration

'Look here,' said Charlie, dragging an old envelope out of his pocket. 'This arrived in the post this morning, and is an invoice from a tour manager for a weekend break.' They had written their fee on the front, put the invoice inside with no explanation, and expected the accounts department to sort it out. 'Well, it is going to the bottom of the pile, and when they phone up demanding their money I will have the greatest delight in telling them how much valuable time they waste with their inefficiency,' Charlie snorted.

So the two tour operators' 'wish-list' included proper lectures on the paperwork that needs to be done – however unpopular with tour managers and guides.

Course contents
All in all, their wish-list for a course included

- transfer procedures
- accommodation check-ins
- conducting walking and coach tours
- how to research for different tours
- how to deliver commentaries for different groups
- environmental issues
- personal awareness
- selling excursions
- administration and paperwork
- problem-solving
- using the mike and your voice
- EU law
- customer care
- body language
- map reading
- marketing yourself and finding work
- getting on with colleagues
- personal grooming
- and if time, running a hospitality desk.

Coming to the end of their wish-list, I noticed that neither had mentioned knowledge. Didn't they need to know if the guide had this? 'Er – well, yes . . . but some guides dish out too much information,' they said. If booking a registered guide, they know that guide will have the required local knowledge, but so often that isn't what they need for today's groups. 'Less is best in my line,' according to Charlie. 'Conference groups want a guided tour tailored to their needs. So point out the relevant sights, then give them time to catch up on gossip. Sitting on the coach may be the only time they have to chat, and that is what they are there for. One of my best guides will give a five-minute introduction on a favourite boat trip, then go around the boat chatting to my delegates. They love her – the women ask about the best shops, the men will come out with a question of local economics, and she makes a mark with every group I ask her to look after. I have noticed her go over to a lone delegate, chat to them and then introduce them to other delegates, so they are no longer on their own.' Sam wanted to know her name, but Charlie wasn't telling. As for Sam, he says he looks for tour managers with specialist knowledge. 'Anyone who has taken the V&A course, or history of art as a degree. I do expect them to have taken a basic course to teach them administration, but after that it is down to charm and "stickability". If something goes wrong, I need to know they will move heaven and earth to sort it out. Teach that on a course, and I'll be delighted to interview the trainees.'

Try before you teach

Alternative Travel of Oxford offer special tours for teachers. These are at the beginning of the season, when prices are much cheaper, but the tour is the same. Teachers can have a good holiday, but see 'how it's done', before they have to teach it.

Talking to Alternative's tour managers, they are a remarkably friendly lot, with a fantastic breadth of knowledge. At their annual party, discussion ranged from enquiries about which dogs one saw on a holiday through Tuscany – Maremmas, according to one tour manager – to Canova's influence on Danish sculptors of the Victorian era. But all told with charm and enthusiasm, which is the hallmark of the best tour managers.

Exams

The English Tourism Council say at least one examiner should be a tour operator. Although it is generally easier to find guides to be examiners, not using employers can lead to problems with candidates feeling they haven't received a fair assessment. There could be the feeling 'I failed because they don't want any more guides taking away work.'

However, NVQs should ensure fairer assessments in future, as long as the assessor has industry knowledge. In some other disciplines, because of time and money, colleges and exam boards have tended to use general assessors, following the principle that anyone can assess anything. However, in tourism this isn't so; an assessor needs to understand the industry, otherwise it could be that they pass someone who may be able to fill in the paperwork to their satisfaction, but actually would be useless when faced with common tourism problems.

Some guide exams in Europe make use of genuine tourists, which makes for much better interaction between exam candidates and assessors. The local tourist information centre advertises exam tours at a cheaper price, and there is usually a mix of visitors and locals, come along to see the fun.

7 Finding work

At the outset

People imagine they will find an ad. saying something like

GUIDE WANTED

Training given by company before you start taking simple day tours under the guidance of a senior member of staff.

It doesn't happen. The reality is that first you have to find a company that is prepared to offer you a job. Valerie was asked by someone to take a tour when she had no experience, but this seldom happens. Finding work is usually a Catch-22 situation; companies want experienced staff, but new entrants find this impossible to get. So they phone and phone, but at the beginning of the season no-one wants to help them get experience.

How to start?

Make use of the jobs lists from your training course. The lists aren't there just to fill up student packs. A good list will have been tried and tested by previous students, although with the way that BT are changing numbers, companies moving, etc., you will find many numbers are incorrect. To find correct ones you can call Directory Enquiries free from a call box!

Before you sign up for a course, ask

- Are there any companies that recruit students from the course?

- Are the tutors part-time lecturers normally working in the industry?
- Will you be given a list of contacts to approach?

Tutors who work in the industry know the companies that are potential employers. They can help you decide where to start.

A good course will have employers phoning to offer vacancies. Usually after the course is ended! But tutors will phone you – so make sure you have notified your tutors if you change your address.

Using your list, look up coach companies. Many offer weekend breaks – a good way to start. You gain good knowledge of areas and venues; then you can apply to tour operators with wider-ranging programmes.

Good training pays off in so many directions, and a recent MORI poll highlighted the value clients place on their dealings with staff. Forget about buzz words such as 'relationship marketing' and 'internal branding', MORI's Director of Consumer Research, Peter Hutton, says it is good, old-fashioned customer care that counts, and gives tourists a happy tour. More important, happy tourists tell their friends, and this is more effective than the most expensive advertising campaign.

However, your first job usually comes from one of the hundred or more names on your lists. And then it is only offered to you because someone has fallen ill (like Theo) and the operator is desperate. You feel your expensive course was a waste of money, until you get on the coach and realize that the admin. details that were boringly dinned into your head, actually are very useful. Without them you would be really stuck. Gradually it all seems to come together, and you realize that what you learnt on the course is coming back – and you are enjoying the work.

Usually you return home raring to go on your next tour. And because you can now say you have experience (without specifying how much) you are offered more work.

Advertising for tour managers

You can find some ads, particularly for tour manager jobs, but they are scarce and there is no recognized media for these ads.

Ask friends and family to keep a look out in the jobs pages of the broadsheets.

Alternative Travel are one company that advertises every January or February in the national press for tour managers and guides. Their ad. asks for applicants 'who are fluent in two other languages apart from English and who enjoy travel, good food and wine, and good company. You must also have a full, clean driving licence'. The advertisement does not give much away, but suggests an interesting job, with a lot of travel involved.

Applicants are sent a form to complete which not only asks for their personal details and work experience, but also poses a series of scenarios to which they must respond. Alternative Travel's staff are not allowed to discuss these forms with potential applicants as the forms are meant 'to give a true indication of the mind-set of the applicant. It is extremely important that the right kind of person is employed by Alternative Travel as each trip leader or manager is a representative of the company's high standards of quality and service'. The company are very proud of the fact that they have won the Investors in People award four years running.

Application forms are read by director Christopher Whinney, who interviews applicants personally. The best applicants are invited to attend a comprehensive residential training and selection week in Oxford, which includes role-playing, as well as practical training in First Aid. The company says 'those applicants who survive the week, and are willing to work, are then offered a position'.

'Willing to work' is the key phrase; many people want to do this job, until they realize the hard work involved.

Finding guide work
The first thing to realize is that you are probably looking for a job in a million. Not because it is exciting and interesting (although most jobs are), but because when you find your job it is very often a one-off. Although there are literally thousands and thousands of people working as tour managers and guides, as they work for very small companies there may only be one or two similar jobs available each year.

So you have to be creative in your job-hunting; one way is to visit the local coach park, and write down the company names and telephone numbers on the back of each coach. Phone these companies and ask if they need people to look after their clients – and you could strike lucky.

Make friends with your local priest or vicar, and you could find you are offered a job taking a pilgrimage to Lourdes or a Millennium visit to Rome. The year 2000 celebrates two thousand years of Christianity, and in celebration of this year and subsequent years, there will be a rise in tours with a religious theme; and no, you don't have to give up your time for free. Vicars have to be commercial today and realize 'the labourer is worthy of his/her hire'.

If you have experience of caring for disabled people, there are many tour operators who would welcome your expertise.

Networking is one of the best ways to find work. Invest about £40 in student membership of ACE (Association for Conferences and Events) and talk to fellow members at events and exhibitions. Conference organizers are always looking for ideas for conference tours – and need the staff to look after them.

Membership of ACE or the Tourism Society entitles you to free entry to tourism exhibitions (normal cost £20). Go round and take note of the hotels exhibiting in your area. After the exhibition is over, phone their conference department and hall porters, and see if they are interested that you live locally and could provide guided tours for their clients.

Sophie's training course had been told very firmly that the regional tourist board were *not* responsible for finding them work. Talking to experienced guides who lectured on the course, they were told that being mentioned in the tourist board's register of guides was no guarantee of work. 'You might get one or two jobs a year from this,' said one tutor.

The trainees were told they had to market themselves, and Sophie's fellow course members decided to go round the local 'tourist' restaurants and see if they had anyone coming to them to ask for a guide. They didn't, but one manager told Robin, 'Wait a minute, X tours come here every week and I know that they are looking for another guide as they want to run extra tours.' And the company were happy to give him his first job.

Gradually the class talked to coach drivers and found more

companies that might want their services. They handed cards out to drivers and hall porters, and offered to help the tourist board for free at a travel exhibition, provided they could also hand out their cards.

Sophie's brother was a whizz with a computer, and that Christmas she found him asking her a lot about her job. Christmas morning she unwrapped an intriguing package of papers, and there were 100 beautifully printed Newsletters giving her details, interests and hobbies in a jokey way, and inside were 'Sophie's Top Tips for Interesting Tours' with ideas for individual tours for groups. That afternoon she mailed the first ten off to potential clients, and by New Year she was already receiving bookings. It was the best Christmas present she had ever had.

Her brother worked in marketing and had been very clever; marketing a tourism service was no different from marketing a thousand other services. Understanding human psychology, he made the Newsletter a 'teaser'. Telling readers enough to whet their appetites, but not enough so they could pass information on to their regular guides and tell them to do the tour.

Getting started

You are now in business – the business of promoting yourself to tour operators and potential clients for your expertise. It is up to you to be as professional in marketing and promoting your services as you will be when in front of visitors.

When going for an interview with a tourist board you are warned that the board can't help get work. But in your enthusiasm you think that jobs will be there. But with so many 'old' guides out of work, you have to offer something unique, and not rely on old-fashioned ideas for tours. These may have worked in the past, but today it is lateral thinking and providing what the visitor actually wants that gets work.

Languages

Everyone expects that in this field of work you need to speak languages. To some extent this is true, but there is work for people who speak only English. It is estimated that 80 per cent of the world's tourism is handled in English. In Romania my guide, Maria, told me that her previous group was from Japan. She gave their tour leader the explanations in English, and he translated this into Japanese.

Valerie says, 'I speak five languages well enough to get by in most situations – but when I started I only spoke English. However, I soon realized that if I wanted the best tours, I had to speak a language. So I taught myself by chattering non-stop to the poor drivers, and constantly referring to a dictionary. Today, there is an easier way – modern technology has come up trumps.

Recently a company called Auralog has received several educational awards for their language pronunciation system. Eva Grynszpan says it's 'a speech recognition system for language training. You sit in front of a computer, put on earphones, and talk to the screen.'

Trying out a course, the screen graphics are funny, and within a few minutes you are answering simple questions; the screen gives you several choices – you speak what you hope is the correct answer, then the screen highlights words you mispronounced. There is a handy graph to help, so you try again, get it right, and the screen goes on to the next exercise. Eventually trainees are chatting away to the screen, and this is a fun way of learning a language.

This is a speech recognition system, rather than language teaching, although as you progress you are learning the language. What it does teach you is how to pronounce words correctly, and for the British who are loath to speak a 'foreign' language this is a boon.

You can choose your own degree of difficulty – from basic to 'mother tongue'. If you can't get a word right, the SETS (spoken error tracking system) graph shows you which word is wrong, and where you are mispronouncing. At the end of each lesson it shows you on screen how well you did – and you are so involved that you are thrilled when the computer awards you good marks! It's a bit like having a private tutor without the embarrassment of having to talk to them. Somehow talking to a computer you don't mind making mistakes – so you are relaxed and are soon pronouncing words correctly.

To use the course, you need one of those 'talking' computers, but if you don't have one, find the nearest child and ask to borrow theirs. They will love the Auralog programme, so there may be a fight as to who gets to use the system! (0207 929 6266).

As a guide, once you can offer tours in a second language this doubles your job opportunities.

Good luck!

8 Interviews

If you network effectively, you are just as likely to be offered a job over a cup of coffee at an industry event as by a traditional interview. However, whether the interview is an informal five-minute chat, or a whole day meeting a company team, here is a guide to help you maximize your chances, particularly for the more formal interview:

- Find out as much as you can about the company before the interview.
- Always arrive early. If delayed, phone to warn you will be late.
- Always look smart and clean. Your appearance is the first an interviewer sees of you.
- Shake hands firmly and look your interviewer in the eye when you meet. Try to maintain eye contact throughout the interview. Don't fidget.
- Be aware of the interviewer's personality and meeting style. Be formal if they are – if they are relaxed, you can be less formal. Just don't make the mistake of being too informal and letting something out of the bag.
- Do not interrupt the interviewer when he/she is talking. There will be plenty of opportunity for you to speak.
- Be honest and don't over-elaborate. If you don't know the answer, say so.
- Give full answers in response to questions. Avoid 'Yes' or 'No' responses.
- Think questions through – don't give hurried answers.
- A smile, a hand gesture (within reason) and your use of voice create an interesting and lively impression.

- Interviewers are human. Whatever you may think!
- Fill out application forms. Yes, you have a CV – but companies want information presented in their way.

Preparation

This is the first essential step towards a successful interview.

- Know the exact location and time of the interview, the interviewer's full name, the correct pronunciation and title held.
- Beforehand, ask for a company brochure and read it through, especially the 'small print'.
- Prepare the questions you will ask. An interview is a 'two-way street'.
- When you arrive (early) be nice to the receptionist. Ask where you can leave coat, umbrella, etc. Don't carry anything you might drop into the interview room.

Common questions at interview

- What interests you about our tours?
- Why do you like working with people?
- What problems have you had with clients on tour?
- How did you go about solving these problems?
- Which days or tours do you enjoy the most and why?
- What are your major weaknesses and what are your strengths?
- What are your hobbies?
- What charity work do you do?

Watch our for . . .

- poor personal appearance,
- poor diction or grammar,
- over-emphasis on money – interested only in remuneration,
- making excuses for unfavourable factors in your record,

- lack of tact/maturity/courtesy,
- condemnation of past employers,
- failure to look the interviewer in the eye,
- limp, fishy handshake,
- failure to ask good questions about the job and company,
- lack of preparation for the interview.
- *Don't* smoke even if the interviewer smokes and offers you a cigarette. Many tours today specify 'no smoking', and even if you can go hours without a cigarette – you will be put down as 'smoker'.
- Nervousness. Everyone worries about this at an interview, but interviewers expect it; they will be impressed if you overcome this. But they dislike aggressiveness, a conceited 'superiority complex' and 'know-it-all' attitude.
- *Don't* 'over-answer' questions.
- The interviewer may steer the conversation into politics or economics. Be discreet.

Once the interviewer has finished talking, you could ask about:

- detailed description of the tour/s,
- reasons why they need staff,
- company culture,
- any training,
- what sort of clients they have,
- company's future plans for tours,
- best-selling tours,
- the next step.

What to wear

At an interview the person interviewing you wants to know if you will fit into the company, and that means the way you dress. Think if you have tattoos or body-piercing. For some jobs you will be identified with the clients – in others they will run a mile.

Men

- A smart suit, preferably in classic navy blue, grey or black, or blazer and smart slacks. No loud shirts. Never jeans. Clients have been known to dislike white socks.
- Earrings and facial jewellery should be taken out if you wear them. Large rings on your fingers should also be removed. Tie your hair back if you wear it long.
- No 12 o'clock shadow. Don't wear too much aftershave.
- For certain companies, cover any tattoos with a plaster if they are visible.

Women

- A smart suit or dress and tights. Be careful not to be too 'trendy'. Shoes should not need reheeling.
- Limit the jewellery you wear. Only one pair of earrings (even if you've had your ears pierced more than once!) and take out any nose rings.
- Take care nail varnish isn't chipped; the colour shouldn't be too dark, and blue makes you look anaemic.
- Use 'day time' make-up. Perfumes should not be too overpowering.
- Pay extra attention to personal hygiene – don't eat garlic for lunch.
- No carrier bags: invest in a briefcase or smart handbag and leave other bags, umbrella, mac, etc. outside the room.

At the end

If the interviewer offers you a job and you want it, accept on the spot. If you wish for some time to think it over, be courteous and tactful in asking for the time. Set a definite date/time when you will provide an answer.

Don't be too discouraged if no definite offer is made. Tour operators will probably put you into the system, and offer work when something suitable comes up.

If you get the impression that the interview is not going well and that you have already been rejected, don't let your discouragement show. Once in a while an interviewer who is genuinely interested may seem to discourage you in order to test your reaction.

Thank the interviewer for the time spent with you. If you really want to work for the company, a courteous letter thanking them for sparing the time to see you, and saying you would like to work for them in the future, can result in an offer later on.

Don't forget, in this industry with 99 per cent of jobs being freelance, you will have to attend many interviews before you have built up enough contacts for year-round work.

To give you a flavour of what a typical tour operator looks for, we asked the secretariat of AITO (Association of Independent Tour Operators) to say what its members look for.

'I think it's fair to say that AITO members probably retain staff for a longer employment period than the larger mass market competitors. This is for a number of reasons. Staff are regarded as important players in small teams, very often working with owners/managing directors and therefore gaining an enormous amount of experience from them. Our members have a high percentage of loyal and repeat customers, and therefore the staff they employ must be able to reflect the reputation of the company.

For many of our members, integrity, loyalty, service and reputation are the key to their success. Therefore, they seek staff who share the same philosophies and approach to customers. As many of our members operate specialist programmes either by destination or by holiday type, they need to employ staff who have an interest or are able to develop an interest in their particular product.'

9 Working with colleagues

Coach driver

You and the coach driver are going to be working 12–14 hours a day together, six days a week, so it is essential you work together as a team.

'If a driver arrives in a grumpy mood, it is probably because he has been working since early morning, cleaning out the coach, and hasn't had time for breakfast,' says Sophie. 'So I treat them like children – get a cup of coffee and a sandwich, and make them eat up. Then they are their usual sunny selves.'

Nothing sexist in this, but most drivers are male. When you see the size of American or Japanese suitcases that a driver has to load into the boot, you soon realize why not many touring drivers are female! Although there are women drivers they mostly drive day tours, although a few do tour for longer.

You and the coach driver have to work as a team. Today, when booking a tour, prospective travellers look at the brochures, and then tot up what is included, generally booking with the company that has crammed the most sights into the legal hours a coach driver can work.

Case study

If you would like to know what is included in an 'average' milk-run tour, get out a map of the West Country, and follow Sigrid and Jim on their way around five of London's hotels, where clients wait eagerly for their coach to pick them up at the start of their tour. It's 8 a.m.; at last everyone is on board, and off they go for the start of the

West Country tour. On the M4 motorway Sigrid will set the scene: telling clients about seat rotation so everyone gets a good view; reminding everyone that if they are ten minutes late back to the coach after a stop this means arriving an hour late at their hotel, etc., then giving clients an outline of the tour ahead.

First stop Stonehenge. Jim grabs a cup of coffee while Sigrid tells the group about the stones. Then off to Salisbury – Shaftesbury – Sherbourne; as it's Saturday the towns are full of shoppers and there are always hold-ups in Honiton. Finally they pull into Exeter, hoping the hotel has the rooms allocated the way Sigrid discussed on the phone.

Look at a map, and imagine Sigrid and Jim at dinner. No time for chat – they are busy going over next day's route, discussing how they can trim five minutes off here – another few minutes there – because the next day is going to be long. No comfort stops next morning as they head off to St Ives, where passengers have a long stop to look around the attractive fishing village and visit the Tate Gallery. Then on to Penzance – Land's End – Marazion – Polperro – arriving at their hotel in Plymouth at 7.30 p.m.

Next day the itinerary is through Dartmoor, going past the prison; Exmoor – Dunster including a visit to the castle, where Jim catches up on much-needed sleep in the coach park, having been up since 5 a.m. to clean his coach – Glastonbury – Wells – Bristol. Another long day, and Sigrid says, 'You'd better get your timing right, and make sure you give exact directions otherwise you lose your people in towns.' The final day they 'do' Bath and Oxford, and drop everyone off back at their London hotels by 5 p.m.

Teamwork is essential. 'You and the driver cannot possibly afford to take a wrong turning' otherwise you can lose hours and everyone arrives in a bad temper, late for dinner. 'Do you want to hear about the Scottish four-day tour from London?' she asked, as she prepared to set off on another marathon tour.

Illegal driver guiding

In the Public Service Vehicles (Conduct of Drivers, Inspectors, Conductors and Passengers) Regulations 1990, the law says:

1) A driver shall not, when a vehicle is in motion, hold a microphone or any attachment thereto unless it is necessary for him, either in an emergency or on grounds of safety, to speak into the microphone.
2) A driver shall not, when the vehicle is in motion, speak to any person either directly or by means of a microphone.

As a guide you will come across the driver who normally does their own guiding. However good a job you do, they are going to be resentful of what they see as you taking the limelight, and 50 per cent of the tips when normally they get 100 per cent. If you are sure of your ground as a good guide, you can say to them that you know they will get a bigger tip at the end of the day with a guide than without. Strangely this is generally true. Human nature being what it is, clients used to the coach driver doing everything will think the job is easy – and reward accordingly. See two people to tip, and often they will give each one the same amount, or even more than usual. After all, they reason, the job is more difficult if it takes two people to carry it out.

So let's hope tour operators cease asking drivers to do the two jobs. Anyway, anecdotal evidence suggests that the coach tours with a driver and a guide book up first, and provide more customer satisfaction and more repeat customers.

Local inhabitants and conservation

To a visitor, a satellite TV dish can be an abomination, ruining the local architecture. To the owner, the satellite dish provides a window to the world.

Sometimes conservation causes more problems than most people would imagine; for example locals cannot understand why animals who have been their food supply for generations, or killed their stock, should be protected just for visitors to photograph.

The tourism industry now realizes that conservation doesn't only mean protecting what we see as the environment, but also understanding local conditions, so that conservation is seen as a benefit rather than a threat to local customs. Every year, more and more organizations are started up to help bridge the gap between what is perceived as ecologically sound practice, and what is needed by local inhabitants.

Concierge or hall porter

These gentlemen (and a few ladies) are often members of the Golden Keys (Les Clefs d'Or) fraternity. This is a world-wide network of people who will help each other help clients. Their symbol is golden crossed keys worn on their lapels, and they work at the best hotels in their area. So-called 'luxury' hotels that don't have a hall porter who belongs to the Golden Keys – aren't luxury hotels at all.

Need tickets for the hottest show in town that has been booked solid for six months? Need a nurse for a sick passenger? Need a document translated? The Concierge can handle this. 'Impossible' doesn't seem to be included in their dictionary.

Generally they will have local town plans to give to your clients, and know where to find shops, and that obscure museum that is of particular interest to one of your group. At the end of your visit, remember they appreciate a tip.

Head waiter

A good head waiter can make your life easier provided you have liaised with them over meal times. When juggling times for several coach groups, liaison is vital. A good head waiter likes to 'dress' their restaurant, putting the smartest and most important people at prominent tables. This can mean you and your driver sitting in full view of your clients, when all you want is peace and quiet. So don't forget to request a quiet table.

Waiters

The waiting staff earn from the percentage they receive on drink sales. Often clients won't order wine as they don't know what to ask for. Always explain to clients which are the local wines, how much they will cost, and which ones go with what food. The only thing your group shouldn't do is drink tap water. No percentage in that.

You have to check menus, to ensure there is a variety. Although your company will have ordered different meals at every stop, if the supplier hasn't delivered what is ordered, the hotel will supply a substitute – usually chicken, as that is a safe alternative. In the height of the season too many substitutions will have your passengers clucking away. Meals for clients usually consist of bland 'International' food designed to be safe as possible for travellers' stomachs. However, if you and the driver want something different such as steak, most head waiters are only too happy to supply whatever you and the driver want. It is customary to give a small tip as a thank you.

Hotel receptionist

You will have checked with the hotel the day before, so it can be irritating to arrive in front of the reception desk to be told 'you're not in the computer'. You feel like replying 'No, there isn't room for me inside', but this is where patience comes in. You will have taken the name of the person with whom you confirmed details; asking for them shows you mean business. They come out from the back, and generally will find the details, and with luck all the room keys already put out in neat envelopes, making it easy to distribute these to your clients in the coach.

If your clients are constantly booked out, it may be because your tour is an 'inexpensive' holiday, with clients paying a low price. Any complaints, and you tactfully draw their attention to the small print. However, this doesn't mean you and the driver should be given sub-standard accommodation, although this can happen. You are both entitled to single rooms with bath (unless warned of no bathroom before the tour starts). Some Continental coach operators' contracts specify the driver must have a room with bath, and even give the driver an allowance for laundry.

You may wonder why tours stay in bland modern hotels with 300 similar box-like bedrooms. Sadly, human nature being what it is, if one couple are lucky enough to have a better bedroom than the rest of the group, instead of commenting how lucky they are, the rest will demand a similar room, even though they have only paid for the minimum standard room. If you arrive at reception to be told, 'One of your group will have the honeymoon suite tonight' – you or the driver sleep there – unless you have a genuine honeymoon couple or someone who has had a bad room whom the group will be happy to see in this suite. You or the driver will keep your mouth shut, and not brag to clients.

Sometimes a client will complain about a room with no justification, often because they are tired or jet-lagged. If possible, keep them away from the rest of the group, so they can't stir anyone else up. Then go to the receptionist and ask if there is another room available – and move them to this. It may be exactly the same size, colour curtains, etc., but the client has made their protest, you have proved sympathetic, and everyone is happy.

House, museum and site guides

When touring, you welcome good house guides. You can leave your clients safely in their hands while you get on with paperwork. In a recent *Holiday Which?* survey, the house guides of Castle Howard (of *Brideshead Revisited* fame) just edged ahead of Chatsworth 'because of the clear explanations about the visit and the friendly and knowledgeable guides'.

However, it isn't always so. Beware when you arrive with your group for a visit to a special venue. You have been told that you have a stop for X minutes. Timings have been confirmed to the venue and you check this with the official venue guide. Then you find that this person has totally ignored timings and throws out your tight schedule.

Or your happy group are changed into a growling, complaining group because they do not receive a good tour. The venue guide makes no attempt to tailor the tour to their interests, and they feel the whole visit is a waste of time. It can take you hours to help them forget this.

Bad house guiding is a problem for tour managers on many tours. The house or stately home is included in the itinerary, so you have to go there. You are not allowed to guide inside, however well you know the property; that is the province of the house guide. After a tour around the building, out come the clients, grumbling at how boring it was, and then complain vociferously, 'Why doesn't your company do something about this?'

The house guide who goes well over allotted time is probably a very good guide, who has your group in the palm of their hand. However, you have a ferry to catch, and when you tactfully try to usher your group out, the guide turns to your group and says, 'Would you like to see so-and-so?' and of course they do. Do you say 'No' and risk unpopularity? Or agree, knowing your driver will have to drive like a fury to catch the ferry? Either way you are going to be unpopular. *Holiday Which?* magazine has called for a national grading system to highlight the attractions with the best site guides and stewards. This was prompted by a survey in which Buckingham Palace was bottom of the league when it came to providing a rewarding day out for visitors. According to *Holiday Which?* 'little effort is made to bring its State rooms to life, and the only way to understand what is there is to buy the £3.70 guidebook'. Mrs Susan Bowen, visitor manager of Buckingham Palace, says staff only have a four-day training course, although 'they do receive on-going training througout the opening period'.

There are some superb house guides, and *Holiday Which?* highlighted the Beefeaters' (yeomen warders) tours, which are rated the best part of a visit to the Tower of London. The warders carry out intensive training, and have to be good guides to be asked to lead the tours.

With a bad guide you have to be very tactful. You can't say what you think, but have to pick up the pieces. You put in a report, but guides 'belong' to the house, and there isn't much the company can do.

Talking to colleagues, they will often tell you about the

house-guiding situation. If the guides are bad, you can tactfully give an overview of the house and its history, so clients have an idea of what to see. If the guides don't keep to time, warn clients that the coach *has* to leave at such-and-such a time, to keep to time. Tell them if they want to shop for souvenirs before they leave they must finish their tour at a certain time. Then when you do your little welcome speech to introduce the house guide, you repeat what time everyone has to leave 'because of safety and keeping to the speed limit'. If this has been explained to them in advance you can find your group surprisingly helpful when the time comes to leave. They troop out *en masse*, and sometimes house guides will get the message. Sometimes!

Other colleagues

Always work with colleagues, even if they are working for rival tour operators. During the height of the season this is essential, particularly in Ireland, where the roads are narrow and a procession of coaches from rival companies travel the same tourist circuit.

Sometimes new tour managers try to buck the system and run tours to their timing. Not only is this unpopular with colleagues – and rivals – but if you arrive at a stop out of sequence, you don't gain any time, but have to wait until the previous group has finished.

Usually tour managers meet up over lunch on the ferry or dinner at the popular tourist hotels, to plan timings for the next day. If you are a new tour manager, you will be expected to take the most unpopular timings. Once you are experienced you call the shots and take the prime times for breakfast, coffee stops, visits, etc.

Beware! If you decide to go it alone and muck up the system, you won't get much help from colleagues, and they can easily make life very difficult for you.

Incidentally, when travelling on international ferries across the Channel the ferry company will allow you to use the lorry driver's restaurant, provided there is room. A coachload of passengers is important to the ferry companies, but one 40-ton truck provides even more revenue – and it will travel 12 months of the year. So to keep their drivers' loyalty the ferries provide superb facilities for HGV drivers. The passengers may eat in a self-service fast-food restaurant; the lorry driver expects an air-conditioned restaurant with tablecloths, a carvery or special 'dish of the day'. Provided there is space, this is where you meet up with colleagues and plan to fit in your itinerary with every other coach.

Crisis management

It is highly unlikely that you will ever be involved in a crisis. But it is as well to be prepared and think through how you would react.

If on a coach, how would you react together with the driver?

How you would react if the driver were injured?

IATM recently published an article on this important subject. As they say, a good tour manager will, by nature, react positively to any kind of disaster. Talking to people who have been involved in accidents, they agree that they reacted to the situation automatically. All agreed that it would be helpful for companies to give them more training and advice.

So what if the worst happens?

Before starting any tour, you should be given a manual explaining what to do and who to contact in an emergency, including death. 'Without the immediate and professional response of their Tour Operator, there is only so much the Tour Manager can do', according to the IATM.

It is of utmost importance that the team back at head office has crisis-management procedures in place. I asked Michael Bland, who trains companies on crisis management and wrote *Communicating Out of a Crisis* (ISBN 0–333–72097–0), to give some pointers:

- There is often no right or wrong way to handle a crisis.
- Tell people what's going on.
- Take a deep breath.
- Be seen to do something.
- Be polite – to enquirers, relatives and press.

- If you have a team and have time – discuss what you are to do.
- Show care and concern.

Learning from crises means thinking through brainstorming sessions on 'what if'. You can't prepare for a crisis by preparing elaborate lists, but can think about crisis-handling by examining other well-publicized crises and asking

- What happened?
- How could it have been handled to give a different result?
- Why did that crisis get the amount and type of publicity that it did?
- How did the management handle it?
- What seemed good and bad about their response?

Michael's tip: the bigger and fatter your manual of crisis procedures, the less people will remember what's in it (if they read it at all).

However, some crisis preparation is essential. While many companies over-prepare in terms of trying to plan for every contingency, most under-prepare by doing nothing and hoping it won't happen. If your company doesn't have procedures in place, one company that advises on crisis management is PR Newswire (0207 454 5115).

Coach accident procedure
If you should be unlucky enough to have an accident, the following procedures were approved with Philip Carlisle at the CPT (Confederation of Passenger Transport).

Take a deep breath – calm yourself – before doing anything.

Then see if the driver is all right.

Then he/she should shut off fuel before helping you to evacuate passengers.

- Help the injured.
- Prevent further accident/s. Keep passengers off/away from road.

- Arrange for driver/walking passengers to call ambulance/ fire/police.
- Put out warning triangles.
- Look after other passengers.
- Inform company.
- Deal with press/sightseers.
- Give walking passengers something to do – it can help them in stressful situations.

You will have to take a lot of decisions and take action all at once. Once the shock impact is over, people will start screaming. Before that happens try to call loudly down the coach to tell people you are coming to help. If they are screaming, *don't worry* – they are alive.

If there is a danger of fire, evacuate as quickly as possible, otherwise keep passengers in the coach until you find a safe place.

Make sure *no-one* goes on the road, however quiet. Emergency services will use it and could run down people milling around.

Once passengers are in a quiet place and fed and watered, if not injured, ask them to let you have statements for your company's eyes *only*. Follow hospital visits procedures if passengers are taken for medical treatment.

If contacted by the press politely tell them you can't take time to comment as your first priority is to look after the passengers. Give them the emergency telephone number of your company.

Reassurance and a sympathetic ear are often what people need most after an accident. And once you have done everything you can to assist passengers, if there is time you should cover up the coach company signs. Cameras will broadcast scenes from an accident, and it doesn't help clients to see the coach company's name in horrendous circumstances.

Handling the media can be fraught with problems. Don't, whatever the circumstances, blame your employer. At least you will get a rap over the knuckles – at worst you could end up in court. When talking to *any* journalist, imagine your boss is standing beside you – don't say anything the boss could object to. And *never* believe any journalist who says 'This is off the record.'

However, 'No comment' is a stupid statement. At best it annoys journalists who are trying to do a job; at worst it gets them imagining all sorts of dreadful events and digging around for any sensational items they can find. A dignified comment that you are sorry for those involved, and suggesting the media contact your company at their emergency number, as you have to do what you can to help the survivors, is probably a good way to handle such a situation.

There is a 'grey area' of responsibility which tour managers and guides should think about. Although there probably aren't any more natural disasters such as earthquakes, floods, etc. than before, TV brings them closer. Sometimes you can't win. One night a coach was parked legitimately outside an hotel at the bottom of an Austrian mountain pass. A van went out of control coming down the pass, and crashed into the coach. Local newspaper headlines screamed 'Coach Crash!'

Look after yourself
If *you* feel a situation is dangerous, don't carry on. Raising questions about safety often gets you mocked by those who may be worried about the situation, but could be paid to carry on regardless.

Time and time again, reading reports on accidents in the media, someone says 'we were worried'. If there is the slightest doubt, trust your own instincts. It's your life. Don't carry on. In many instances a good check is to ask to see insurance papers. It is surprising how the Jeep-safari operator or boat-trip owner fades away when you ask for official papers.

10 Working with clients

Normally when people go on holiday, they are in a good mood. However, flight delays or jet-lag can upset them, and turn them into the Clients from Hell.

We are not talking about 'air rage', but nasty verbal exchanges and complaints about your company as clients take out their feelings after hours stuck in a crowded, over-heated airless plane cabin. You have to be prepared to accept that this will sometimes happen and deal with the situation calmly and courteously; if you can't, then this job isn't for you.

However, these ranting, raving clients will turn into the nicest people once they have had a good night's sleep. However, 'Once a season, I get the group from hell,' says Valerie, 'and there is nothing you can do but grin and bear it – do your job professionally and keep your head down until they leave.'

Even with the nicest group you are constantly walking a tightrope, which is one reason why you don't become *too* friendly. A flippant remark about a trivial incident can suddenly make your happy group think you are an unfeeling monster. However, you have to ensure that you talk to every one of your passengers every day, even if it is only a sentence or two.

Clients can object to what you wear. Your clothes have to reflect the type of company you represent. If the company offers a party-mad ravers' scene, you dress accordingly. However, the majority of people who will be taking tours are middle-aged couples, so you reflect this by dressing conservatively (with a small 'c'). Off duty you can wear the latest gear – sitting in the front seat you have to give an impression of neatness and efficiency.

One of the strangest aspects of this job is loneliness. You

would think that being surrounded by people, you had a ready-made circle of friends. T'aint so.

Being at the top is lonely. You are in charge of a coach-load of clients, and to keep your authority you have to keep a certain distance. Your word is law – and you may have to make an unpopular decision to keep to a timetable. Every time you tell your group it is time to get back on the coach, when they would much rather stay on the vine-shaded terrace overlooking the stupendous view, you are making a small but unpopular demand of them. Although you are a friend to everyone on the coach, you have to be careful not to spend more time with one couple than with other clients – however much you get on together.

Tourism Focus, the magazine of Tourism Concern, recently had an issue devoted to tour managers and guides. Veronica Wallace, from Scotland, talks of the need for 'cultural insight, sensitivity and empathy to respond to culturally created questions' such as 'why are drainpipes on the outside of houses?' and 'why so many chimney pots on the roof'?

You have to have an enquiring mind. Yes, you need to know about history and geography, but your clients will remember the 'fillers' you use to enliven your commentary. Pointing out the milk bottles on doorsteps – long since gone in most countries; mail delivered through our front doors – not having to be collected; and the fact that Britain doesn't have the country's name on its stamps because we invented them. Money is also interesting: there are Florins in the UK, Netherlands, Czech Republic, etc., because their banking systems came from Florence; Netherlands money is designed to be user-friendly for blind people, and so on.

All the time you have to remember you are the bridge between visitor and local. You have to be the buffer of anger, misunderstanding and resentment from both sides, and sort out problems with charm and tact. Sometimes these problems will make you think and understand much more of people's cultural differences: in *Tourism Focus* Corinne Attwood who takes tours to China was quoted as saying that 'Chinese people were particularly shocked when an elderly widow travelling alone died at the start of a tour to China. They wanted to know how could her family have let her take this risk? Why didn't she want to stay home with her children and grandchildren?'

All the time you are on your own. Friendships take time to nurture, and yet all your friends at home will see of you is a few hours in between tours. You will make friends of colleagues, but you tend to talk 'shop' when together, and you can't escape from your job. In the summer season you may return home at night absolutely whacked and all you want to do is crash out – to be ready to leave home again at crack of dawn the next day. The time to see your friends is in the winter – so make sure they realize this, and are still around.

There are some clients that will take over a tour, loudly claiming that 'everyone' wants to do this, or go there. You have to walk a tightrope between listening to their demands while ensuring that everyone – including the quietest – gets to see and do what they have paid for.

Health problems

Anyone looking after tourists should be trained to administer basic first aid. One of the commonest problems is handling possible heart attacks when 5,000 feet up a mountain pass. Americans in particular only have a limited holiday time; they rush through preparations, take an overnight flight and then go sightseeing as soon as they arrive in Europe. By the time they reach their first mountain pass it's not surprising their over-loaded heart sends up protest signals. That's where first aid training comes in very useful, until you can call up the ambulance.

Upset stomachs are common on tour; tonic water is often very useful in such situations.

Never ever give clients any tablet or pill. You are not a doctor, so how do you know that they won't react? Even if they say they always take a proprietary brand of medicine, local manufac-turers can have different strengths for example and if anything goes wrong you could be sued. If they need something you take them to the nearest chemist, where they can ask for this themselves. By the same token, if they fall over and the slight graze can be cleaned up with an antiseptic wipe, you hand this to them to use; *don't* do this yourself.

Oranges should be banned from coaches. When people complain of motion sickness it is often after eating oranges. Doctors will tell you there is an acid in an orange that can cause problems when travelling, and the smell is enough to make some people sick. And it bears repeating that it makes sense to try and keep the coach toilet locked, unless there are special circumstances.

Tipping

Nina from Norway couldn't understand why we were so coy about tips. 'If someone wants to give me one I say thank you.' Remember, too, that in some countries the drivers are taxed on a notional amount. If your driver doesn't get a tip, he or she will still have to pay tax. You may not need the extra money, but they will, so it is up to you to ensure that they get their tip.

Valerie says she tells her group that she has been asked by some members what is the usual tip for the driver. She says she can't answer this, but if the group want to thank X for the wonderful job he has done, the local custom is to put the tip in an envelope and he will appreciate this very much. This also cuts out the client who makes a collection 'for the driver', and then pockets his own percentage – it happens.

Remember, clients that shout loudest don't necessarily tip. And Australians are notorious for saying 'We had a marvellous tour, but we don't tip back home.' When in Rome . . .

Commission from excursions, etc. should always be shared 50/50 with your driver. There are some people who think themselves above their colleagues, and insist on taking more. Surprisingly they don't seem to earn as much as those who quietly share.

If you have a city tour, remember to tell your clients how much to tip the local guide; it is only a small amount to each client, but spread over 40 people it makes a difference to the guide. If you get your clients in the way of tipping, even small amounts to porters and chambermaids, come the end of the tour and you won't have to say anything for the driver – and you! Clients will work out how much they have given a city guide 'for only a morning', and you should each receive a respectable amount. Well, most times. There are always the exceptions.

'I always know how good the tip will be by the envelopes.' According to Valerie, clients will start to ask hotel receptionists for envelopes two or three days before the end of a tour, in which to place their thank-you letters and a banknote. 'The earlier the requests, the better the tip.'

Timing

Timing is extremely important. Restaurants may have other groups to accommodate, and you arriving late means others will have to wait. If you ask your driver to pick you up in a crowded area, make sure your group are waiting on time. The mark of a bad guide is the driver being told by traffic wardens to move on to allow other coaches in.

Cultural differences show up in this area, from those nationalities who consider it rude to be late – and can't understand arriving at a restaurant and the tables aren't ready – to those who so enjoy visiting a country that they don't mind taking extra time over their visits, and have to be tactfully told the coach driver has to keep to his hours. Tachos (tachographs) can be helpful in keeping clients to time, if you explain what they are – or ask the driver to do this. Tachos are specially coated paper disks that the driver inserts into the timing clock on his dashboard. These accurately record times, distance travelled, stopping times and speed, so if a driver goes over his legal driving hours limit this shows up on the tacho. It helps to explain to passengers how tachos work; people with an analytical mind are interested, and it helps to explain why you insist on keeping to time. Also, if the police stop your coach to inspect tachos, passengers are intrigued rather than frightened.

Tachos are examined minutely for infringements by the transport ministries of most EU countries. Generally the driver has to keep his tachos for the past fourteen days, showing days off and days worked; the police have the right to see these. At the end of this period these tachos are sent off for analysis to an official centre. In the unlikely event of an accident the tacho provides vital evidence.

Academy of Culinary Arts

Thanks to the efforts of innovative and mega-hardworking chefs, food in British restaurants is no longer a joke. There is some innovative and delicious cooking going on, but as the restaurants are frequently off the beaten track they are difficult to find. One golden rule: if full of locals, the cooking must be good!

If you look after groups that are serious about their food, in Britain there is an association of famous chefs, food providers and gourmets called the Academy of Culinary Arts – similar to the Academie Culinaire in France. Their secretariat is a mine of information; Sara Jayne Staines produces a fascinating newsletter which often features a list of London members offering pre-theatre menus in Michelin-starred restaurants at virtually half price.

The Academy is working in conjunction with Baxters – yes, those people who make the soups your passengers buy at lunch in the Woollen Mills in Scotland – to improve the quality of training and food appreciation (0208 874 8500).

Curry or pizza are supposedly Britain's favourite foods, but visitors want fish and chips, roast beef and Yorkshire pudding, steak and kidney pie and all the other delicious foods which used to be staples of our diet. If you want to know where to find 'real' British food for your groups, contact Food From Britain or the Academy. Food from Britain provides publicity for British food and co-operates with various regions to promote British food in campaigns such as 'A Taste of the South East', 'Heart of England Fine Foods', 'Welsh Food Promotions' and 'Tastes of Ulster'. Look for stickers and ask tourist boards for lists of participating restaurants (0171 468 8579).

11 Making life easier

Work within the law of the country you are in. Don't be tempted to break the law to help your clients. Do you want to lose your job?

If a passenger is detained at Immigration, in most countries there is usually a valid reason. If the problem is not of a client's making, then follow your company's guidelines.

In the old days, tour managers had very little legal protection. The media carried horror stories of tour managers being imprisoned as collateral until tour operators paid their bills. Today, this shouldn't happen in most countries. The EU Directive has done much to clean up some of the illegal practices of dodgy tour operators, and staff are much better protected. However, there are still some rogue companies around, so if you are asked to do anything suspicious, *don't*.

And don't be taken in by the little old lady who finds out you live in the same town as her nephew – the present she asks you to take for him will certainly contain something that could see you behind bars for a long time.

Today, tour managers are more likely to fall foul of local legislation that says only locally registered guides are allowed to accompany groups in certain situations. To make sure you don't land in trouble:

- Never guide a group in an area where the law obliges you to have a local guide. It's not fair on you or the guide. For example, some British operators still ask their staff to guide in Paris. They should book a local guide.
- Carry copies of your certificate translated into the

language of the country in which you are working, to prove that you are qualified to accompany a tour.

Recently there has been much discussion over the definition of 'tour manager' as opposed to 'guide'. Originally tour managers were often called 'couriers', but Brussels has decreed that this term applies to parcel couriers. At a meeting to discuss NVQs, the guides' representatives agreed that couriers should be called 'tour guides', and many colleges now offering NVQs, such as York, use this definition.

However, nothing is simple, and recently 'new' definitions were agreed by the CEN Working group (European committee for standardization) CEN/TC 329/WG2: Tourism Services – Travel Agencies and Tour Operators. We have used these in Chapters 2 and 3 – but the CEN definition still doesn't stop tour operators calling staff anything from courier to tour director – and tour guide – and meaning a person capable of carrying out the same tasks; incidentally the starchy Foreign Office still uses the objectionable word 'escort' for the staff they send to meet VIP guests! On definitions, a recent letter stated 'it should be noted that, although the terms have been agreed by the CEN working group, they are still under study and subject to official verification'.

Valerie seems to have the right attitude: 'As long as I enjoy my work I don't mind what I am called.'

Channel tunnel

Opening the Channel tunnel has helped increase traffic across and under the Channel to record figures. Rather than diluting existing traffic, its high profile and ease of use increased awareness and traffic.

Eurotunnel is proving a rival to the ferries, causing these to upgrade their services. Eurostar has changed the composition of tours. US, Japanese and Australian groups now go one way by Eurostar on the 'milk run' around Europe. Incentive conferences are big users, and the train's convenience has opened up northern Europe to the British weekend and day-trip market.

Some ski tour operators are now sending groups by train from the UK to the Savoie region in France, and they need train tour managers to look after clients. Clients are happy to avoid the delays and jams at Geneva or Lyon, which can make train times compare favourably with air travel. If changing trains, this is a seamless operation at Lille; bliss for tour managers!

Lille is fast becoming the most popular station on the line. The city is a tourist delight, and if going further travellers find it easy to transfer between trains, so opening up northern Europe. Most TGV trains pull in on the opposite side to Eurostar's platform, so you just have to transfer your group about ten metres.

As an antidote to so much surly service on today's transport, Eurostar's crew earn top salaries, which shows in their dedication and the way they look after groups. However, one golden rule is that the check-in time is twenty minutes before departure. Arrive after this, even with a group, and you can't get through.

Eurostar is constantly upgrading services, and if you have a group booking it is worthwhile checking that you can have the following facilities: exclusive carriage; dedicated check-in if needed; choice if meal booked (N.B. on the Disneyland visit it is always a cold main course); drinks service. On the Gold First Class service they supply return coach transfers, which could save on French coach hire costs. Telephone for the group booking office is 0870 6000 777. Special services 0207 928 0660.

Any problems, and tour managers speak fondly of the efforts made by train managers to sort these out. One Friday evening a train manager suggested taking a group to Waterloo Station's main entrance, rather than try for taxis at the Eurostar exit – saving a half hour wait.

Warning – if going via Brussels to Ghent there are no lifts at Ghent station; instead a long hike up and down steps. However, try and route your group via Lille and get a coach to pick up there for the short journey overland to Bruges or Ghent.

Flying

Forget about cramped, overnight charter flights. Looking after groups you fly with the big boys – generally on scheduled services. You will still be seated in cattle class, but it has two or three inches more seat pitch (the amount of room between seat edge and back of seat in front) than charter flights. And short-haul scheduled flights fly during the day.

Your group can be delayed, like anyone else, but treat the check-in staff right, and you will know much more of what is going on. A sympathetic approach, and offer to take your group away from their desk, can produce a fast offer of refreshment vouchers.

When checking in, Valerie says, 'I always ask to be seated away from my group. The cabin crew are there to look after them. But more important, if there were an accident, sitting in the middle of the group they will look towards me to see what I say, rather than pay attention to the cabin crew. I have seen it happen, and it could mean the difference between life and death'.

Sigrid says that flying time is when you update paperwork, but even so cabin crew can interrupt to ask for assistance when it is a cabin service matter. However, the upside is that when she flies to pick up a group, she is often upgraded to Business Class.

Generally, if you fly by the airline of the country they will have a dedicated person whose job it is to look after groups. Services vary, but provided you phone the day before, most will offer advance preparation of boarding passes and a dedicated check-in desk. While others are still queuing, your group will be inside the duty-free area.

The following numbers are for group services at airports. Phone in advance, giving as much warning as possible to ensure you get the seats you want for your group, and airlines should be able to arrange

- dedicated group check-in desks
- pre-allocated seating for groups of 20 or more
- boarding passes

Alitalia   London – 0208 745 8468. In Italy fax details to Milan
– (+39) 2–74865008; Rome – (+39) 6–656335427.

Austrian Airlines   London – 0208 754 8594; Vienna – (+43) 1
7007 654 82.

British Airways   say they need 48 hours notice to try to ensure
passengers are seated together: Heathrow Terminal 1 – 0208 562
7707; Terminal 4 – 0208 562 9450; Gatwick – (01293) 666409.
   If luggage gets misrouted (never say lost!), BA's Arrivals
Services are heroes with 'misrouted' bags – 0208 562 9231.

Emirates   offer extras such as
   • Group baggage tagged for easy identification upon
     arrival.
   • Meet – and – assist service available if group are con-
     necting from a different airport.
   • Welcome announcement made by either the captain or
     other crew on board.
   • Facilities for using personal telephones and fax machines
     on board. They were pioneers of inflight telephony.
   • And, as they charmingly say: seated with spare seat if
     available or if necessary in a different class. Now that's
     worth knowing.

Heathrow – 0207 808 0019; Dubai – (+971) 4 494 204.

KLM and KLM-UK, Northwest and Brathens   UK – fax 0208
750 9090; Schipol – (+31) 20 648 7426; USA – (+1) 800 645
9696.

Lufthansa   London – 0208 750 3490; Frankfurt – (+49) 69
696 944 33.

Swissair   London – 0208 754 8594; Geneva – (+41) 22 799
3230; Zurich – fax (+41) 1 812 9030.

Turkish Airlines   London – 0208 745 0109; Istanbul – (+90)
212 663 0709.

In-flight phones are installed in most scheduled carriers today. For the moment the dreaded mobile phone can't work up in the air, so phone-freaks have to buy time from the airlines – and do they charge! However, if you need to change reservations or make an urgent call they are worth their weight in gold. Most phones are installed in the backs or arms of seats in business class. Economy class probably has phones at the entrance.

In-flight telephone operation is relatively simple, although it can help to have a child explain the finer points. Jetphone are one of the largest 'carriers' in Europe, and can arrange to have calls charged to your mobile phone number. Currently phones can only make calls from air to ground, but Jetphone are working on technology to enable travellers to receive calls from ground to air. Some airline cards will give you a discount on Jetphone calls.

And in-flight phones have other uses. Jetphone say a customer used an in-flight phone to call the airline's customer service centre (on the ground) for a gin and tonic. They called the cabin crew – and one thirsty passenger ignored by cabin crew duly received his drink.

Railways

Eurostar is mentioned in the Channel tunnel section, above. Whatever the papers write about British railways, tourists love our trains, particularly the Great British Breakfast, but do pre-book if optional.

To check group bookings, wheelchairs, porterage, etc., phone: Gatwick Express – 0990 30 15 30; GNER (the line to Edinburgh) 08457 225 225; South West Trains (to New Forest) 0845 605 0440; Silverlink has a marvellous new service from the North to Olympia and Earls Court – (01923) 207818; for other lines phone National Rail Enquiries – 0345 48 49 50.

French TGV: Lille-Europe – (+33) 3 28 55 80 67; Paris-Nord – (+33) 1 55 31 54 68; Paris-Lyon – (+31) 1 53 33 69 85; Nice – (+31) 4 92 14 82 66.

Travelling by Swiss Railways is almost as convenient as having your own coach. There are usually plenty of trolleys, and any booking office will give you a print-out showing where you change, to which platform, how many minutes you have to transfer, and what refreshments are available on the train. The restaurant cars are delightful. A limited but delicious menu is served at round tables, which make for a fun journey.

Making a claim

A sad fact of life is the number of times you will have to accompany clients to the police station to report theft. You must do this within 24 hours of an incident. Theft can happen to you as well as clients, so always carry a copy of your insurance policy: it will have helpline numbers and what to do in an emergency. For lost or stolen goods, having the original proof of purchase will help you claim, especially if it is a new item. For lost or delayed luggage, get a PIR (property irregularity report) from the airline.

Keep all receipts for any expenses incurred, especially for medical treatment.

Money

Credit cards can be used in over 240 countries; the major ones are Mastercard, Visa, Amex, JCB, etc. Visa kindly provided this checklist, which applies to all major credit cards, and say the following points should be repeated to clients at the beginning of any tour.

- Treat your cards and travellers cheques as carefully as you would cash.
- Don't keep all your methods of payment in the same place.
- In crowds, hold your bag or wallet close to your body.
- Consider using a safety deposit facility at your accommodation.
- Regularly check you have your card(s) and travellers cheques.
- Photocopy your passport, tickets, cards and visa (where applicable) and keep these records separate.

- Take contact details of relevant embassies, high commissions and consulates.
- Keep your eyes on your card when paying for goods and services.
- Check the information on the sales voucher is correct – you are liable for the amount written in the total box, so make sure this is filled in before you sign.
- Protect your card's magnetic strip from other cards and objects, especially if magnetic; if your card is damaged it may not be accepted in electronic terminals or cash machines (especially in France and Italy).
- Take care when using cash machines, make sure that no-one attempts to discover your PIN.
- Carry card insurance and let the company know *immediately* if your card is lost or stolen.
- Exchange rates – card foreign exchange rates tend to be better than local tourist rates.
- Keep a copy of all sales vouchers in order to check them against your statement when you return home.
- Tell clients to request a written quotation from merchants as additional proof of the agreed price (in case there is a different amount on card statement).
- Always keep your travellers cheques and sales advice slip separate so you have a record of the numbers in case they are lost or stolen.
- Take small-denomination travellers cheques – to avoid having to carry around large amounts of cash.
- Keep a record of where and when you cashed your travellers cheques, and the serial numbers in case of loss.
- If travellers cheques are lost or stolen, contact the appropriate refund service immediately.
- Do not countersign your travellers cheques until you cash them in the presence of the encasher.

Visa say that in France you might have problems having your card accepted. The phrase to use is 'Les cartes Britanniques ne sont pas des cartes à puce, mais à piste magnétique. Ma carte est valable et je vous serais reconnaissant d'en demander la confirmation auprès de vôtre banque ou de vôtre centre de traitement.'

Additionally some UK-issued cards now contain a chip, but they do not operate like French chip cards. They should be accepted by reading the magnetic stripe. If cardholders do experience problems they should ask the retailer to contact their authorization centre: 'Certaines cartes émises en Grande-Bretagne sont munies de microprocesseurs (cartes à puce) mais ne fonctionnent pas comme les cartes françaises (pas d'utililisation du code confidentiel pour le paiement). Elles doivent donc être acceptées par lecture de la piste magnétique. Vous pouvez appeler votre centre d'appel pour vérifier la validité de la carte.'

Thomas Cook will supply a Tour Manager's Priority Card; show this at their bureaux and you don't pay commission when changing money. Contact Eva Pakula on 0207 908 4260.

Trouble-spots

The Foreign and Commonwealth Office Consular division's Travel Advice Unit on 0171-238 4503/4 gives the latest travel advice and information on trouble-spots to be avoided.

Health

Things that bite

Lying on a hot bed, being driven mad by insect bites is one of the worst aspects of this job. Nasty creepy crawlies are everywhere, from Scotland to South America. Mosquitoes are becoming more resistant to preventative measures, and it is imperative that if you are going anywhere near them you should

- take appropriate precautionary medicine,
- wear clothes that cover as much of the body as possible,
- slap on products designed to protect your tender skin.

Many companies make insect repellent; some more effective than others. One that is in many tour managers' bags is Jungle Formula Insect Repellent; it is sold in Boots, including their branches at airports, and has been effective in keeping these little xxxxxxxs away. The same company also make a wasp repellent, and extra-strength Jungle Formula for expeditions.

Don't forget this if you are working in Florida (lots of mosquitoes around) and Scottish Highlands (ditto midges).

Vaccinations

There are other dangers to travel – typhoid, polio, hepatitis and other diseases lurk waiting to infect travellers. Don't think that just because you are holidaying in Europe or a 'clean' country you are not going to catch something.

At Unilab in London, Maria deals with travellers from all over the world. She has a computer in which she inputs information from returning travellers, and she and her colleagues were some of the first to highlight to risks of diphtheria and tuberculosis surfacing after the fall of the Iron Curtain.

Maria's advice is to go to a specialized clinic for advice; some doctors don't have the necessary specialized knowledge. Maria says she has recommended certain vaccinations to students, and told them to get them at their doctor's as students may get concessions. Then she finds doctors say these aren't necessary. But they are.

Returning on the same plane as someone from a high-risk area can see an unsuspecting traveller ending up with a nasty dose of some 'exotic' disease. Read the local newspapers abroad; often they carry a small paragraph listing notifiable diseases – the ones you should be protected against. On second thoughts, don't – unless all your jabs are up-to-date.

Vaccinations don't hurt! At least Maria doesn't! Make sure you get an International Health Certificate; carry this in your passport at all times. The Medical Advisory Services for Travellers Abroad (MASTA) also provides tourists with specific information on the latest health risks abroad. Their 24-hour Traveller's Helpline is 0891 224100. Unilab (0207) 908 722 or (01276) 685040 can give information on the nearest clinic.

12 Why don't we . . .?

Or, Ideas to make your tour that bit special

With the EU Directive making life difficult for any leader who wants to inject a bit of individuality into a tour, today it can be difficult to give visitors that extra something they will remember all their lives.

Travelling through the Alps, if you were lucky when autumn came, your hotel might tell you tomorrow was the *descente des vaches*, when the cows are decorated for their trip down from the mountains. You could ask your group if they would like to forgo a baroque church or two, and go off to watch. Now, the Directive says brochure itineraries have to be followed – otherwise clients can sue a company. So bang goes spontaneity.

However, if you are asked to help design a tour, the following are some ideas from the 'special drawer'.

Countryside

Britain has wonderful countryside, yet tours seldom take advantage of this, or give foreigners the chance actually to mingle and meet genuine British people. Visitors have all seen photos of the men in our Royal Family playing polo, and there are over 50 polo grounds around Britain where groups can watch this sport. Phone Hurlingham Polo Association (01869) 350044, for details.

The top polo club is Cowdray, in Sussex. Next to the Argentinian Open, the Cowdray Gold Cup is the most important championship in the World. During June and July Lord Cowdray's private estate is the venue for superb High Goal matches, where visitors mingle with the locals watching exciting tussles. After the excitement, everyone socializes over a Pimms or a glass of champagne. It is even possible to arrange seats for your group in the private members' stand – (01730) 813257.

Sheepdog trials take place all over Wales, the Lake District and Scotland throughout the summer. Farmers and country folk take part in sports such as Cumberland wrestling (where they wear thick white tights!) and show off local crafts, while watching, and commenting freely on dogs exhibiting their skills. The BTA can send a list of trials.

Cultural kingdoms

On the way from London to Edinburgh, coaches roar through the ancient Kingdom of Northumbria, an area that is sadly neglected by tour operators. Want to stay in a Castle? This is the place. Want to get away from tourists – take fascinating walks – or see ancient Roman forts? It's all here.

There are local ground handlers who specialize in looking after up-market groups. A typical tour gives your group drinks in a Pele Tower and then they dine in one of the castles used in the film *Elizabeth* in front of a roaring log fire. After dinner a local tells spine-chilling ghost stories – all great fun – (0990) 50 2220.

Eurostar

Going under the Channel is an exciting option for a day out from London, and Eurostar has excellent promotional fares for groups. Only two hours away from London, Lille has everything – and then some. The Musée des Beaux Arts is the second biggest in France, and has a wonderful collection of paintings by Goya and others.

Eurostar station is a little out of the centre, but an inexpensive taxi transfer of five minutes sees you to the heart of the pedestrianized district. Here you will find Patisserie Méert and their speciality waffles, so delicious that when Lille's favourite son, Géneral de Gaulle, was President, he insisted on a weekly delivery.

Vera Dupuis at Lille Tourist Office is a model of a good

tourist officer. Ask her for ideas for a day trip for your group and she will organize everything from a demonstration of tying a Hermes scarf to a 'shop till you drop' ramble in and out of designer boutiques with their 'must have' clothes – cheaper than Paris. She recommends a visit to the museum to see their fantastic collection of model relief maps which cover a huge area of the basement. Secure in their glass cases, these relief models of the major northern European cities two centuries ago were so accurate that they were used to train spies.

Her colleague, Delphine Bartier, covers the Nord Département in the attractive countryside outside Lille. She is another enthusiast with bags of fresh ideas; particularly helpful if you want to organize anything from children's tours to gourmet meals. She has organized a superb antiques trail for visiting groups, and managed to find some incredible bargains that had dealers buying.

Asked to recommend a restaurant that was big enough to take 45 people, without losing the atmosphere of a small French restaurant, Delphine recommended L'Ecume des Mers. Run by Antoine Proye, scion of a famous restaurant family, this restaurant is in the heart of Lille's old town, with a vast seafood menu. Huge plates of *fruits de mer* will have your group's eyes starting out of their sockets, and menus cooked by the chef Christian Leroy start at £15 a head. Eurostar – 0870 6000 777; Vera Dupuis – (+33) 3 20 21 94 30; Delphine Bartier – (+33) 320 57 59 59; L'Écume des Mers – (+33) 320 54 95 40.

London for free

The milk run taking in Westminster Abbey and the Tower is expensive and overcrowded. But there are many other venues that are free, fun, interesting and unknown.

If you have to waste time on the way in from Heathrow before hotel rooms are ready, why not make a short stop at Hogarth's house – the cartoonist whose ideas were used for the welfare state? Then there is the British Museum; the Bank of England Museum – where you can see gold bars, and learn lots of fascinating facts for your own commentaries; Kenwood House with its magnificent pictures; the Arabian fantasy of Leighton

House; the National Army Museum; the National Gallery and National Portrait Gallery next door; the Royal Hospital, Chelsea, where your group can meet up with those delightful old soldiers; and the Wellcome Trust near Euston Station with interactive models showing how our bodies work.

More ideas? Phone LTB's Travel Trade Helpline on 0207 932 2015.

Prague

Charlie had to organize a special pre-Christmas lunch for a company who wanted to go to Prague for the day. Airtours run day tours there in winter, so the flight and sightseeing were taken care of, but where to lunch? 'I looked in my trusty Relais et Chateau hotel guide, and there was the Hotel Hoffmeister. Relais et Chateau is a marketing consortium with high standards – I use their member hotels and restaurants with great success.'

Restored since the fall of communism, the hotel is within walking distance of the Castle, and was the home of Adolf Hoffmeister, a noted film director who used to draw caricatures of his friends: Dali, Cocteau, Picasso, and the like, and get them to sign these. His son is now in charge, another son produces food from the family farm, and Hoffmeister's caricatures are displayed all over the hotel; you lunch in an elegant art gallery. Hoffmeister – (+420) 2 5731 0942; Airtours (01706) 240077.

Trentino

Whizzing down the A22 between Innsbruck and Venice, you drive through the Trentino region of Italy. This region has everything – castles, gourmet food and wine. Five minutes off the motorway at Rovereto is the Ristorante Novecento – ((+39) 464–435 2220). The owner has his own vineyards, and when I lunched there with a group of wine writers they actually bought bottles to take home – very rare!

Many of the vineyards you can see from the autostrada welcome groups and can often organize a guided visit, wine-tasting and food: Ca'Vit – (+39) 461 381 700; Conti Bossi-

Fedrigotti – (+39) 464 439 250; Distilleria Marzandro – (+39) 464 435 595; Gaierhof – (+39) 461 658 514; Istituto Agrario di San Michele all'Adige – (+39) 461 615 252. Many of these also make *Grappa*.

The capital city, Trento, has the famous castle with frescoes, fables and a fascinating history of the Council of Trent. Shopping is excellent, and handbags are often cheaper than in Florence. For small groups the restaurant Due Spade is *the* place. For larger groups try the garden restaurant of the Hotel Academia; a favourite haunt of international film stars.

The castle forms the backdrop to a series of festivals widely patronized by the locals, but worthwhile investigating for groups that want to hear international artists without the crowds and prices in Verona.

The tourist office publish excellent literature. Phone APT Trentino – (+39) 461 497 350.

Turkey

Turkey is a new country when it comes to tourism, and there are still teething troubles. Local guides insist on standing up as the coach bowls along, 'so you can all see me', and are so used to the lower end of the market that they have been known to say, 'You have five minutes to see Perge before we go to the carpet store.' Coaches have 'no telephone' signs, but drivers don't think this applies to them – until you forcibly remove their mobiles and tell them to concentrate on driving. Beware the Jeep-safari excursion – many insurance companies say it is highly unlikely clients are insured.

Trying to return to Perge, I was lucky enough to meet Fethi Pirinçcioglu, Chairman of VIP Tourism. Within five minutes he had arranged a superb guide to take us back, who not only explained in simple terms the difference between Greek and Roman architecture, but pointed out early adverts and said, 'You can see they had traffic jams 2,000 years ago – look at the wheel ruts.' Fascinating.

Turks are welcoming and charming, starting with Turkish Airlines and their in-flight magazine; it always has a really good article on some aspect of Turkish culture, with lots of information for commentaries – and even lists the calories in the on-board meals.

In Istanbul there are many restaurants serving a 'Night with the Sultan' meal of Turkish cooking: dolmas, shish kebabs, etc. Yes, this is genuine, and delicious, but based on peasant cooking. To really eat as the Sultans would have eaten, book your group into the Tugra Restaurant at the Ciragan Palace Hotel . The menu is a work of art, with exquisite calligraphy on special paper. The dishes live up to this, and the chef has researched into old cookbooks to serve what the Sultans would actually have eaten. Dining looking out onto the Bosphorus, it's an experience. Ciragan Palace Hotel – (+90) 212 258 33 77; Turkish Airlines – 0208 745 0109; VIP Tourism – (+90) 212 233 64 84.

TV tours

Way back in 1968 a company called DEAL wanted to give visitors a fresh look at London. Realizing that the TV series *Upstairs, Downstairs* was being shown on TV from Russia to Australia, they devised a tour taking in places used on location. This was an instant success.

When Lord Zetland's company, Dundas International Conferences and Promotions, offered TV tours to British coach companies, they just 'grew and grew'. *Last of the Summer Wine* tours hit the top of the popularity league, and there were tours from *Poldark* country to London locations.

The BTA estimate that the blockbuster films *Rob Roy* and *Braveheart* produced £15 million extra in tourist revenue for Scotland. TV and film location tours are so popular that the BTA have published a Movie Map showing locations used from Broughton Castle, used in *Shakespeare in Love*; Osborne House filmed for *Mrs Brown*; Sheffield, of course, for *The Full Monty*; Chillingham Castle in Northumberland featured in *Elizabeth*; Notting Hill – where else? – and Bebington Oval on Merseyside, which doubled for the Paris Olympic Stadium in *Chariots of Fire*.

Walk on the wild side

How many visitors say they want to get out and see the countryside, but actually would soon founder if they had to walk in genuine woods? For these, help is at hand from the Forestry Commission. All over Britain they have set out easy-access walking trails, many wheelchair friendly, and ideal as a basis for group tours.

Designed to give visitors an enjoyable experience of our woodlands, these trails are generally short, waymarked walks, leading from a car park or visitor centres with self-service restaurant.

Forestry Commission Rangers often lead guided walks high-lighting different aspects of the countryside. It is surprising what treasures wait down in the forest; during the mushroom season Peter and Valerie Jordan of the Tasty Mushroom Partnership in Burnham Market, Norfolk, lead fungi forays in Thetford Forest. Peter advises clients, 'Don't be greedy when you go mushroom-ing. Only pick enough for a meal and walk away,' leaving enough for others. During their forays, cut mushrooms are always carried in open-weave baskets, with the cap down to allow spores to drop out. Don't pick immature specimens because identification is often difficult, and don't place edible mushrooms with unidentified varieties in the same basket as spores travel.

Phone the Forestry Commission's information line to find the nearest trail, car park that takes coaches, and visitor centre restaurant with room for a group – 0131-314 6322; or 0131–334 0303 for free copies of their interesting magazine *Forest Life*.

And for those times when you are stuck:

Airport delays

Don't despair – enjoy! Clarins are opening up Beauty Studios at airports; wonderful places to relieve stress and spend time during a delay. Instead of fretting, men and women can be pampered with facials, massages and fake tanning treatments. You can have mini-treatments at Heathrow in Terminal 1 airside and full treatments at Gatwick South airside.

WAMWorld

If you've lost your passengers, particularly the males, they are probably in front of the WAM screen. When faced with delays, find the nearest bank of screens (now at more and more airports), and let your passengers play with the touch screens. Each WAMWorld consists of a public TV screen showing commercials, a private interactive screen (complete with printer and credit card reader) and an LED.

Today, a curious and screen-literate public has ensured that this concept is very popular. Clients can find out what to buy at the airport, order products, and even enter competitions.

13 Working from home

In this industry, you are probably a freelance running a business
– yourself. You have to market yourself in order to get work.
You will also have to keep records. This means you need a home
office, and modern gizmos to help you.

Before buying any gizmo, ask:

- How easy is it to set up?
- How good is the Helpline?

Computers versus typewriters

Personal computers, email and the Internet may have become a
way of life for millions of us – but the humble typewriter is still
around. Don't think you are out of the Ark if you still use one
to write invoices. Phil Jones, of Brother, says, 'Many people
predicted typewriters would become obsolete when PCs first
arrived in the 1980s, but here we are at the end of the century
and we're still selling thousands every month.'

Buying a computer, beware ads offering 'cheaper this –
cheaper that'. You are going into a jungle, and unless you know
your way around your best bet is to

- ask a friend who really understands computers to help
  you,
- Go to a major store or company with a good reputation
  and pay for their expertise and after-sales service.
- Alternatively, find a reliable person who can build a
  computer to your specifications. Ask if you can contact
  a satisfied customer.

Cameras

If you carry a camera, remember you will probably need to insure it separately. Some guides lecture on local history and sights to groups, and then take them sightseeing the next day. Tour managers sometimes use slides for welcome meetings. Don't worry if you aren't a photographer. Olympus Cameras say a small zoom camera should be more than adequate, provided you use professional quality slide film. You can only buy this at shops with fridges, and you must keep the film in the fridge at home.

Fax machines

Email can be too time-consuming – you can arrive back for a 12-hour stopover between tours, and find over 100 messages from hotels and other advertisers – which you have to wade through in case one has important information. Many tour managers prefer to have a fax; you pick up faxes and take them around in your hand while checking details. Many major hotels have a location map fax-back system.

The days of fading faxes will soon be over. Technology is reducing the price of alternatives, such as in the Brother 920 plain paper fax, which will store incoming faxes if your machine runs out of paper. More and more companies now fax tour details, and this is often your contract, so a plain paper fax is a good investment (0845 60 60 625).

If you arrive home to find a message that a tour has been cancelled, use your fax to get more work. Symantec make a WinFax Pro which allows you to do fax scheduling directly from your computer, without having to print out. With this you can send the same message to all the companies you work for, telling them you are available. The machine sends these faxes out automatically while you go and have a bath! It even redials if a line is busy. You can also have automatic notification of incoming faxes via your mobile phone or pager while on tour (0207 616 5600).

Phones

There are probably your most important business tool. You must be in communication with employers, and have a reliable message service. However, before you sign up to one of the 170+ companies that offer cheap calls, take a look at their services.

Cable and Wireless have a good policy on offering refunds if customers have a genuine complaint. Both Cable and Wireless and BT's fault repair services work 24 hours a day. Not so with many cable call providers; in order to offer cheaper calls something has to give – usually in the engineering department.

Shop around for call deals, but remember the after-sales service too. Cheap weekend calls are probably not much use; you need to ask what is call cost Monday to Friday during office hours; as a guideline Cable and Wireless quoted UK-Link package calls at 2p a minute locally, 3.5p a minute nationally. (0800 092 0636)

BT offer some very useful services at low prices, such as Call Waiting: waiting for an important call, you can chat away knowing that you will be alerted when it comes. They also offer a different ringing tone for business or friends. (0800 002 800)

Cordless phones
Calls from a cordless phone cost the same as from an ordinary phone. You can carry this to the front door, or into the garden, or even do the washing-up while talking. Make sure the phone is digital for clear reception. BT produces the Quartet 2015 and Diverse phones. Alan and his colleagues on their 0345 697 330 helpline are incredibly helpful.

Mobile phones
Mobile phones – not to be confused with cordless phones – are essential for tour managers. Many tour operators are now insisting you have a mobile; they pay for the calls, but you have to buy the phone.

Make sure your phone can be used in whichever country you work. Ian Volens from OnetoOne says that the minimum you need is dual-band capability for Europe; this will work in France, for example (where there are three providers). However, the bigger and more sparsely populated a country, the larger the void areas. If you are working in USA, you should have a phone with tri-band capability that will tune into 900, 1800 and 1900 frequencies. Although more expensive, tri-band capability will maximize your roaming options.

There are many cheap deals with mobiles, but before signing up ask who makes a mobile phone. OnetoOne are rigorous about the ones they recommend. For advice on international roaming phone BT – 0800 33 33 00; Cellnet One – 0808 100 4111.

Warning: it is illegal to use mobile phones on an aircraft, and that includes leaving them switched on. One passenger found out the hard way when he refused to turn off his phone in a plane. Although he wasn't making a call, he was jailed for a year.

Another warning! Recently Graham Dene, star presenter on Magic Radio, broadcast that he had paid in advance for call units for his mobile. Then the telephone company went out of business. So he phoned OFTEL to ask, 'What are you doing?' OFTEL give out licences, but says companies don't have to be licensed (of course this company wasn't).

Money

It is always a problem to find funds when setting up on your own. Most banks will offer 'starter packs', but when it comes to loans these are very difficult to find.

The Prince's Trust might be able to help if you are aged between 18 and 30 and have been refused by a bank. (0800 842 842)

Euro

The BTA has published a guide to assist small tourism-related businesses. Phone 0208 846 9000 for a copy.

Legal advice

If you want to start up your own business, your local solicitor probably won't know enough to unravel the complexities of the EU Directive on Package Travel. So it is well worth while investing in a session with an expert who can tell you what you need to start up: licences, bonding, etc. Alan Bowen was voted Travel Solicitor of the Year, principally because he has helped so many companies with legal advice on travel issues. So many questions poured into ABTA's offices on the Directive that he produced a *Guide to the Package Holiday Regulations* (£25), (0208 908 1795).

National Express

If you have to travel to pick up a group, or for an interview, don't forget National Express has a network of inexpensive scheduled coaches across Britain – 0990 01 01 04. And the driver might know of other job opportunities.

ANTOR

And finally, ANTOR (Association of the National Tourist Office) in Britain publishes a booklet listing local contact telephone numbers for tourist offices. These get you through directly to the appropriate department, rather than having to hang on spending a fortune on a premium number. There are similar associations in most countries.

Tourist offices can provide basic literature, give you telephone numbers of hotels and restaurants, provide lists of tourist information centres on your route, and sometimes help when you are trying to research historical facts on a new route. (0207 494 0549)

14 Looking after yourself

You are on your own, and looking after yourself is vitally important. You are going to find that you are working all hours – so unless you have good stamina and health, don't start.

Skin care

In this sector your skin is likely to suffer from wind, rain, dry air and pollution, so skin care is vitally important for men as well as women. Dermatologists stress the importance of using creams to protect the skin at all times, winter and summer. Not only to guard against the sun's rays, but also to protect your face and body from pollution. Sadly, before people realized the dangers, working in tourism meant it was easy to get a deep tan, and today many people have skin cancer to show for it. Experts may say 'only' 2,000 people a year die from this in Britain; surely that is 2,000 too many?

Even if you don't think this will happen to you, to get a tan you have to burn your skin – which can't be good.

If you take tours to Australia you will know that they are very concerned about the sun; even the macho Bondi Beach lifeguards now cover up and slap on the protection cream. In Britain men and women are starting to take more care of their skin.

Marie works at Heathrow Airport's Beauty Centre, advising both male and female staff and travellers. For adequate protection against the sun, she says 'look for a minimum SPF (skin protection factor) of 15. And two lots of SPF8 creams do *not* add up to SPF16.' Experts say SPF30 is probably as high as you need to go. Working in tourism means it is easy to find the best products for your particular skin type, in stores, pharmacists and especially at duty free shops. Most products have no smell, so men can use them too.

Travelling around, tour managers have difficulty finding newspapers. CNN is a good way to catch up on world news, but it doesn't give you the feature articles on skin care. This is probably why whenever Michelle does in-house training for tour operators, she says the session on 'Looking After Yourself' is by far the most popular.

Asking colleagues with good skins (one is 70) what worked for them, they all mentioned products from the companies that spend on research, rather than the 'glamour' companies. In many shops if you say you are a tour manager you will be given trial sizes of the products mentioned.

One interviewee had such bad skin that she went to a dermatologist; his prognosis was 'it's your age'. So thinking, 'If anyone has good research facilities, it must be the Swiss', she asked for advice about 'tour manager skin' from Natalie of La Prairie. Naturally Natalie said she should try some of their creams. Why? 'Because these are cellular-based which helps the skin to perform its own natural action more efficiently. As your skin cells begin to deplete when you get older, these are replenished by the La Prairie products.' In plain language, these help make healthier skin.

OK – the proof of the pudding . . . etc. The tour manager's skin is back to normal, and airline cabin crew were probably the first people in the travel industry to 'discover' these products – men as well as women. Cabin crew suffer from lack of moisture in aircraft (a big factor in jet-lag), and these products helped skin after long flights.

Ecologically based compounds make sense, and Sisley produce a useful moisturizer for travellers, which you cover with a Botanical Sunblock with a SPF20 protection factor for a sun-tanned look, and a Restorative Cream which is particularly useful when flying or where your skin suffers from the atmosphere; if you have caught the sun, use this to combat redness.

Roc's Professor Voorhees is a skin specialist, and he has helped develop products for sensible skin care for frequent travellers. Roc Santé Soleil's lip salve and odourless self-tanning cream are particularly popular.

If travel pollution makes your skin break out in fine lines, try Prescriptive's PX range, which includes a Comfort Cream which prevents that horrible tight feeling you get on a long flight. One tip – use Comfort Cream before you get on the flight as a preventative, and on the coach it is a good idea to use it at lunch as well as in the morning. Skin dries out during the day, particularly with a coach's air-conditioning.

Guerlain's Terracotta range produces an incredibly natural suntan look, giving you confidence to face the most problematical group!

And finally, you must rub off that rough skin on the face and body that comes with travel. Strange, but true – except the experts call it exfoliating. Why? According to Una Polke, sales manager for Clarins Travel retail division, 'Pollution, stress, central heating, etc. prevent our skin from functioning as efficiently as it should. When travelling, skin gets dehydrated. Using an exfoliator on the face and body helps to get rid of all the dead skin cells, helps cell renewal and firmness of skin, and allows the products you apply later to absorb and work better; self-tanning products will go on 100 per cent better and give a more natural 'tan'. You should exfoliate on a weekly basis.

At many BAA airports, you can book an appointment with skin consultants, and if you are in a hurry you can pre-order tax- and duty-free goods on 0800 844 844.

Antiseptic wipes

During the season you often get spots all over your chin. Usually these come from germs picked up from the microphone head. Each time you use a mike, wipe it with an antiseptic wipe to disinfect the head.

One final tip: drink plain water. This is vital for skin, and was one of the most popular anti-jet-lag tips from everyone.

Insurance

When you are ill abroad, it is almost useless to rely on Form E111, supposed to guarantee you free medical treatment in EU countries. Even if you find someone who understands the form, it only guarantees basic care, and is no use to ambulance drivers. But every hospital and clinic understands the plastic cards issued by medical insurance companies.

Insurex Exposure specialize in insurance for business travel, and their CEO, Albert Kemp, warns that if you have a personal travel insurance policy it should include *business* travel, not just holiday trips. Today, Albert says medical insurance is vital, even when just working in Britain. And make sure that repatriation insurance is included – that is when the company pays to fly you home if you are too ill to travel on an ordinary flight.

Losing luggage is a problem at any time, and many company policies will only pay a maximum of around £500 when you lose your worldly goods. Look at your company's policy, read the small print that says how much you are insured for, then go through your suitcase and list how much it will cost to replace the items. It will probably give you a shock to realize how under-insured you are. And if an airline loses your luggage you will probably get an even smaller sum (under the Warsaw Convention). So top up insurance yourself if necessary.

You can also take out insurance for loss of earnings, which as a freelance is vital.

Currency conversion

At Thomas Cook Bureaux de Change and on board cross-Channel ferries, tour managers in charge of a group can often change currency without being charged commission. Apply to Thomas Cook for a Tour Manager's Card.

If you lose cash you will probably find that your insurance doesn't cover this – or there is a premium. So many tour managers put their float in the bank, and use their credit card for making purchases on behalf of their tour operator. Keep your statements showing what it cost to change your float, and claim this on your expenses.

15 Associations

ACE

The Association for Conferences and Events has an inexpensive student membership (about £45 p.a.). You receive their *Yearbook*, with information about potential employers, a monthly *Newsletter* with Job Spot and items that should spark off ideas for potential jobs, and an opportunity to network and meet organizers who might need you to look after their delegates. (01480) 457595

AITO

Traditional holidays are declining. People want more contact with locals and more to do. 'Milk run' tours have fewer clients, and recently several large British incoming tour operators that only offered these tours have closed or been taken over. The AITO type of tour operation is set to increase.

AITO (the Association of Independent Tour Operators) is an alliance of smaller, specialist companies dedicated to providing a quality product, personal service and choice to the consumer. The majority of AITO members are small, owner-managed companies that have been banging the drum for conservation, and now find that their clients appreciate this. With their money safeguarded by bonding, clients are happy to trust these lesser-known operators, and it is well worth studying their brochures to see which way tourism is going. 0208 607 9080

BITOA

The British Incoming Tour Operators Association was founded when ambassadors were concerned about industry-wide problems. A gathering of 50 of their client companies at the London Tourist Board gave birth to BITOA, which now represents major incoming tour operators handling individuals and groups into the United Kingdom. They publish a list of members (free) which can provide a useful list for contacts. 0207 931 0601

Coach Drivers Club

Yes, I know the name suggests it's not for you, but . . . members receive an excellent monthly magazine of interest to everyone in the industry, and alone worth the subscription. The club organize excellent Familiarization Trips, where you get to network with potential employers. You also have a chance of tapping in to their insurance scheme – tailored for work in this area. (01454) 273573

Guide associations

If an area or region has official guides, there is usually a guide association such as Scotland's STGA. Started in 1959, but transformed into a company limited by guarantee in 1966, with backing and funding from the Scottish Tourist Board, Scottish Enterprise and Highlands and Islands Enterprise, they are very helpful to enquirers like myself. Currently they have four branches: Aberdeen, Dundee and St Andrews; Edinburgh; Lothians and the Borders; Glasgow, West and South West Scotland and the Highland and Islands; and they offer Ordinary, Associate and Student membership.

There is a similar association in Wales, and elsewhere in Britain ask your regional tourist board for information. In London, there is the Association of Professional Tourist Guides, and the Guild of Registered Tourist Guides (who may be forming an Institute). Abroad, ask your ministry of tourism, or regional or national tourist office.

IATM

The International Association of Tour Managers welcomes tour managers in their first season as Affiliates. There are some very thoughtful committee members who are concerned with taking the industry forward, and their *Newsletter* is a good read. There are various categories of membership; full members have to prove they have worked in the industry for some time. 397, Walworth Road, London SE17 2PQ. 0207 703 9154

Tourism Concern

An organization 'for people who care about the quality of tourism, linking people with things to say to people who can use their information to tell others to actively change the industry'. Annual fee is £18, which includes subscription to their *Focus* newsletter.

Tourism Society

This is particularly useful if you want to start up your own business, as they run an excellent series of evening seminars on important tourism business topics. 26 Chapter Street, London SW1P 4ND. 0207 834 0461

16 Stocking your bookshelf

Any tour manager or guide worth their salt will have a large library for research. You also file brochures and leaflets from tourism venues for the time you are suddenly asked to take a tour there.

Books

This is a list of books recommended by the professionals. There are some unusual selections; all are useful in some way. I haven't included the usual guide books as you can find these for yourselves, but you may well discover they do not give enough information for commentaries. That is why *you* have to research, research and research.

So why not use the Internet? Recently there have been frequent apologies in newspapers due to the fact that information obtained off the Net is inaccurate. Unless you know who has placed the information, it is better to research historical information, dates and facts at your local library. Use *Encyclopaedia Britannica* and books for research. You *must* be sure of the facts you are going to tell your clients, and generally information written in a book has been checked by an eagle-eyed editor.

The *Blue Guide* books are usually accurate and informative and a good basis for commentaries. The *Companion* books often have interesting background information and give you a flavour of the area. However, *beware* guide books for backpackers. Some have a rather inaccurate viewpoint, and what interests backpackers may not interest your clients, who are paying for informed and cultured advice.

Golden Rule: borrow a guide book from a library *before* you buy it. If after reading you realize it is going to be useful, then go out and buy your own copy.

AA City Packs cover major cities. These can be slipped into your pocket and are generally written by foreigners working in the city, so cover the items that will interest your groups. By the side of each description is handy logistical info. Around £5.99 each.

AA Trucker's Atlas tells you where you can and can't take a coach.

ABTA's Guide to Working in Travel is a *basic* introductory book if you want to know more about other jobs in tourism. ISBN 1-900140-49-7, £5.99. (01483) 727321

Airline Passenger's Guerrilla Handbook by George Albert Brown. On lots of tourism industry bookshelves, including their solicitors. Lots of information to be stored away for the time when you have a problem. ISBN 0-924022-04-3, £8.95.

Blue Guides published by A & C Black in London and W. W. Norton in New York. Forget the trendy, backpackers' Bibles. These books have the facts and will be referred to time and time again during your working life. There are *Blue Guides* to most of the popular destinations around the world. Some are better than others, depending on the editors, but they are usually excellent.

Careers in the Travel Industry (Kogan Page) is another *basic* introduction. £8.99.

Cassell Concise Dictionary. You will be using architectural and historical terms which won't be in a PC spell-checker. Cassell's dictionary has useful definitions from 'AA' to 'Yurt'. ISBN 0-304-34779-5.

Cultural Gaffes Pocketbook, by Angelena Boden. She is the co-author of the ETC's 'Welcome Host International' course, and has a fund of amusing anecdotes on different cultural attitudes and expectations. ISBN 1-870471-43-1.

Dictionary for the Tourism Industry. Gives definitions of all those initials, jargon, industry-specific words, etc., and has a very useful section on 'Expressions' to make your talks more interesting. ISBN 0-9527-5090-2, £9.99. 020 823 8800

Getting Into Tourism (Trotman) is my third *basic* introductory selection. £8.99. ISBN 0-8566-0459-3

Good Guide to Britain (Ebury Press), 891 pages packed with information about places to visit. Essential to find space for this reference book on your shelves if you are taking Round Britain Tours. Info. on attractive villages, unusual places, where to eat, entrance fees and tel. nos. ISBN 0-09-186354-6, £14.99.

Handbook on Working at Conferences and Events (Worksaver Publications) ISBN 0-9519611-8-7, £15.

Here We Go, by Harry Ritchie (Hamish Hamilton). A fearless exposé of the last place on earth visited by travel writers: the Costa del Sol. A must for anyone who has watched in disbelief as passengers disembark at Gatwick wearing sombreros and shorts on a typical freezing summer day and will help you laugh at yourself when you are just about to murder your clients. ISBN 0-241-13321-1, £14.99.

Hollis Press and Public Relations Annual. If you want to work at exhibitions or events, you look up names of companies that might have stands. They also publish a *Sponsorship Directory*, useful for events, and *Hollis Business Entertainment*, with details of corporate hospitality companies. 0208 977 7711

Intermediate Textbook for GNVQ Leisure and Tourism (Addison Wesley Longman) a good basic guide to the tourism industry, especially useful if you are setting up your own business. Explanations on tachos, EU Directive, health and safety. ISBN 0-582-27841-4, £14.99. (01279) 623623

Maps – keep these with you *always*. Never trust that your driver will have a map. In Britain the AA's *HGV (Heavy Goods Vehicle) Atlas of UK* – for all those minor roads where you don't know if bridges can take a coach. Leisure maps published by tourist boards and Ordnance Survey maps or similar, showing churches, stately homes, etc. AA, *Collins* or similar maps for Europe.

The *Traveller's Handbook* by Caroline Brandenburger (Wexas). Written by well-travelled people, giving useful information which may help when you have a problem. ISBN 0-90580207-1, £14.95.

The Unemployables by Chris Lewis (Management Books). Just to give you heart – as you read about Marco-Pierre White, Bob Payton, Will Carling, Sir John Harvey Jones, etc., who all found it difficult to find a job at first. ISBN 1-85252-225-9, £9.99.

Willlings Press Guide lists 8,000 newspapers, magazines, etc. Useful to look up which are the local newspapers if you want to trawl through coach company ads, and also if you want to find out the in-house magazines when you have a specialist group to take on an incentive tour, to an exhibition, factory visit, etc. 0208 977 7711.

Working in Conservation Free careers fact-sheet supplied by the UK Institute for Conservation. 0207-620 3371 or (01274) 391056

Working in Tourism. Vacation work. Lists of tourism companies around the world. Covers working in every aspect of tourism from looking after VIP tours to starting your own company; how to find the work and get started. ISBN 1-85458-133-3, £9.99. (01865) 241978

Magazines

ACE Newsletter (members only). (01480) 457595.

Careerscope. (01276) 21188.

Conference and Exhibition Factfinder. 0208 340 3291.

Conference and Incentive Travel. 0208 943 5000.

Corporate Entertainer. 0208 248 7711.

Exhibition Bulletin. 0208 313 0244.

Group Leisure Vermont Place, Milton Keynes, MK15 8JA.

Group Travel Organiser. 0207 735 5058.

Leisure Management. (01462) 431385.

Museums Journal. 0207 250 1837.

On the Road. (01628) 526287. This is the magazine for tour managers, with up-to-date information on coach parking, frontier problems, shopping, and all the little problems that face tour managers. Subscription £15 p.a.

The Organiser. 0207 284 2133.

Travel GBI. 0207 729 4337. This newspaper is an excellent round-up of what's new in Britain.

TTT (Travel and Tourism Training). 0207 823 8800.

17 Helpful contacts

Some associations now charge for information as they don't have staff to handle enquiries. If an association makes no charge for supplying information, please send an s.a.e. Contact your regional tourist board for local contacts for courses.

ACE (Association for Conferences and Events), Riverside House, High Street, Huntingdon, PE18 6SG. (01480) 457585. (Information pack £15.)

AGCAS (Association of Graduate Careers Advisory Services). 0161-272 4233.

AITO (Association of Independent Tour Operators), 133a St Margaret's Road, Twickenham, TW1 1RG. 0208 744 9280.

Alan Bowen. 0208 908 1795.

Arts Council of Great Britain. 0207 333 0100.

Association of Professional Tourist Guides. 0207 717 4064.

BAA Information Line. 0800 844 844.

BASI (British Association of Ski Instructors). (01479) 810407.

BITOA (British Incoming Tour Operators Association), 120 Wilton Road, London SW1V 1JZ. 0207 931 0601.

Bord Failte (Eire Tourist Board). (+353) 1602 4000.

Business Link. 0345 567 765.

CAA (Civil Aviation Authority). 0207 379 7311.

Career Development Loans. 0800 585 505.

CENTFAC (Centre for Education and Training in the Countryside). (01926) 412427.

CERT (Eire state tourism training agency). (+353) 1855 6555.

CILT (Centre for Information on Language Teaching). 0207 379 5134.

City and Guilds of London Institute (NVQs). 0207 294 2468.

Civic Trust. 0207 930 0914.

Coach Drivers Club. (01454) 273573.

Council for National Parks. 0207 924 4077.

Countryside Commission. Publications Dept. 0161-224 6287; Gen. Info. (01242) 521381.

CPRE (Council for the Protection of Rural England). 0207 976 6433.

Department for Culture, Media and Sport. 0207 211 6200.

DfEE Learning Direct. 0800 100 900 (can locate a course or a training provider).

East of England Guide Training, Pam Peterson, 17 High Green, Telegraph Lane East, Norwich NR1 4AP.

English Heritage. 0207 973 3862.

English Nature. (01733) 455100.

English Tourism Council. 0208 846 9000.

Environment Council. 0207 824 8411

Environmental Training Organisation (01452) 840825.

ETOA (European Tour Operators Association). 0207 499 4412.

First Aid Courses – see under Red Cross or St John Ambulance in local phone book.

Forestry Commission. 0131-334 0303.

Green Globe. 0207 930 8333.

Guild of Registered Tourist Guides. 0207 403 1115.

IATM (International Association of Tour Managers), Central Office, 397 Walworth Road, London, SE17 AW. (0207 703 9154.

Insurex Insurance. (01892) 511500.

Irish Travel Agents Association. (+353) 1679 4089.

Isle of Man Department of Tourism. (01624) 686843.

ITMA (Incentive Travel and Meetings Association). 0208 892 0256.

Jersey Tourism. (01534) 500743.

Learning Direct. 0800 100 900 (details on distance learning and other courses).

Leisure World Training Company, 34, Gibbs Road, Banbury OX16 7HJ. (01295) 273574.

London Tourist Board. 0207 932 2039.

Ministerial Forum on Business Tourism. 0207 215 1079.

Museum and Galleries Commission. 0207 233 4200.

Museums Association. 0207 608 2933.

Museums Training Institute. (01274) 391056.

National Business Language Information Service. 0207 379 5131.

National Express. 0990 808080.

NHTV (Netherlands Institute of Tourism and Transport Studies), Sibeliuslaan 13, 4837 CA Breda, Netherlands. (+31) 76 530 22 03.

Northern Ireland Tourist Board. (01232) 231221.

Northumbria Tourist Board. 0191-375 3018.

OCR [Oxford, Cambridge & RSA] **Examinations Board.** (01203) 470033.

OCR Course. 0207 351 4434.

Orkney Guiding Services. (01856) 811 777.

RADAR (Royal Association for Diability and Rehabilitation). 0207 250 3222.

Royal Commission on Historical Monuments. 0207 973 5466.

Royal Geographical Society. 0207 589 5466.

RSA [now OCR] **Tour Guides Diploma.** 0207 351 4434.

Scottish Tourist Board. 0131-332 2433.

Scottish Tourist Guides Association, Old Town Jail, St John Street, Stirling FK8 1EA. (01786) 447784.

Scottish Vocational Education Council. 0141-248 7900.

Sports Council. 0207 388 1277.

Springboard. 0207 497 8654 (an agency with some information on jobs in tourism).

States of Guernsey Tourist Board. (01481) 726611.

Tourism Concern, 277 Holloway Road, London N7 8HN. 0207 753 3330.

Tourism Society, 26 Chapter Street, London SW1P 4ND. 0207 834 0461.

Tourism Training Organisation, South Lodge, 308a Fulham Road, London SW10 9IG. 0207 351 4434. (For information on training courses, books, etc. send s.a.e.)

Travel Training Company, The Cornerstone, The Broadway, Woking, GU21 5AR). (01483) 727321. (ABTA's training company.)

UCAS (Universities and Colleges Admissions Service). (01242 222444).

Victoria and Albert Museum Courses. 0207 938 8638.

Wales Blue Badge Training, 54 Allt Yr Yn Road, Newport, NP9 5EB.

Wales Tourist Board. (01222) 475291.

World Travel and Tourism Council. 0207 838 9400.

Yorkshire Tourist Board. (01904) 707961.

Glossary

bump when a client is off-loaded or denied a seat on an aircraft because of overbooking by the airline

gateway main international airport or port of entry into a country

milk run a traditional, 'beaten-track' tour

pax passenger(s)

tacho tachograph: a device for recording speed and distance covered by a vehicle

Index

Academy of Culinary Arts   103
ACE   77, 131
adventure tour guides   16
airport delays   120
Airtours   117
AITO   85
Alternative Travel   19, 72, 76
antiques couriers   35
ANTOR   126
APL   47, 52, 58
Architectural Dialogue   57
Association of British Professional
   Conference Organisers   59
Auralog   79, 80

BAA   129
Beamish Open Air Museum   30
Bint, Catherine   32
BITOA   132
'Blue Badges'   24, 50, 52, 65, 67
Bowen, Alan   70
Brother Machines   122–3
BTA   115, 119, 125
Buckingham Palace   27, 92

Castle Howard   91
CCTV   68–9
CEN/TC   329/WG2 105
Channel tunnel   105
Chatsworth   91
City & Guilds   55–6
coach accident procedure   95

coach drivers   86
Coach Drivers' Club   132
coach tour guides   14
commission   101
computers   122
Confederation of Passenger
   Transport   95
conferences   15, 33, 59, 71
conservation   88–9
couriers   105
credit cards   110
CREST   7
crisis management   94
cycling tours   16, 19, 28

diploma   7
Disability Discrimination Act   51
driver guiding   88

Eiffel Tower   10
Eindhoven   18
English Nature   28, 59, 60
English Tourism Council (ETC)
   47, 50, 54, 72
EU Directive   62, 70, 104, 114,
   126
Eurostar   5, 13, 18, 38, 62, 105,
   106, 109, 115–16, 142,
Eurotunnel   105
Evans, Campbell   36
Evershed, Allen   11

fax machines   123
ferries   93, 94, 105
first aid   45, 49, 100
flying   107
Food From Britain   103
Foreign and Commonwealth
    Office   112
Forestry Commission   28, 120,
    140
Form E111   129
French TGV   109

Gatwick Express   109
GNER   109
GNVQ   56
'Green Badges'   24, 50, 65
Griffiths, Sigrid   86, 106
guest lecturer   35

hall porters   89
head waiters   89
health and health problems   112,
    116
Hellyer, Dave   29
Holiday Which?   27, 91, 92
hotel receptionists   90
hotels
    Ciragan Palace   119
    Hoffmeister   117
house, site, museum and trail
    guides   42, 91
house guiding   92
Houses of Parliament   30
Hurlingham Polo Association
    114

IATM   13, 14, 20, 46, 49, 56,
    64, 94, 133
immigration   104
incentive conferences   15, 105
in-house guides   23

Institute of Tourism and
    Transport Studies (NHTV)
    48
insurance   42, 110, 111
Insurex   130
Internet   51, 134
interpreters   30
Ironbridge Gorge   30

Jersey Tourism   64
Jetphone   109
Jordan, Peter and Valerie   120
Jungle Formula   112

La Rosière   60
languages   78
legal advice   126
Leisure World Training Company
    20, 47, 50, 64, 141
Les Clefs d'Or   89
Lille   106, 115
loans   63
London Tourist Board (LTB)
    64, 117, 132, 141
London Transport Museum   63
Longdown Dairy   32

marketing   69
MASTA   113
mid-season blues   43
Minzly, Mary   15
MORI   75
Mutual Recognition of
    Qualifications   7, 20
Mutuality of Qualifications   48

National Express   126, 141
National Trust   23
Netherlands College of Travel and
    Tourism (NHTV)   64, 141
New Forest   29, 32

Northumbria   115
Northumbria Tourist Board   64
NVQs   47, 48, 50, 51, 52, 56,
    58, 64, 65, 73, 105

OCR Certificate   7, 12, 20,
    48–9, 50, 53, 55–6, 61,
    64–6
open-top buses   26
oranges, dangers of   101
Original London Walks   28
Orkney Guiding Services   64

Paterson, Jane   30
phones   124
Pirinccioglu, Fethi   118
police   110
Prague   117
press officers   36
Prince's Trust   125

railways   109
regional guide training   54
regional tourist boards   63
registered guides   24
Relais et Chateau Hotels   18, 117
riding tours   16, 19, 28

safety   97
Scottish courses   67
Scottish Guides (STGA)   53,
    65–6, 132 , 142
Shrewsbury Quest   31
Silverlink   109
site guides   27
ski guiding   32, 60
S/NVQ   45, 47
South West Trains   109
specialized courses   57
Staines, Sara Jayne   103
standing up, dangers of   68

step-on guides   35
Stickland, Raymond   29
Swan Hotel   35
Swiss Railways   109
Symantec   123

tachos   102, 103
Thomas Cook   112, 130
timing   67, 102
tipping   101
Tour Managers Certificate   7
Tour Manager's Priority Card
    112
Tourism Concern   99, 133, 142
Tourism Society   77
Tourism Training Organisation
    49, 63, 69
Tower of London   92
trail guides   28
Travel Training Company   55,
    63
travellers cheques   111
Trentino   117–18, 133
Turkey   118
Turkish Airlines   118
TV tours   119

vaccinations   113
Victoria and Albert Museum
    (V&A)   72, 142
Visa (credit card company)   110,
    111,
volunteers   63

Wales   53
walking tours   16, 19, 28
Welcome All (qualification)   50
Welcome Courses   47
Welcome Host (qualification)   50

Yorkshire Tourist Board   64, 143